# LAND OF THE MORNING CALM

A. JAMES GREGOR is a professor of political science at the University of California, Berkeley, and principal investigator for the Pacific Basin Project of the university's Institute of International Studies. He is the author of numerous books, including, for the Ethics and Public Policy Center, *Arming the Dragon: U.S. Security Ties With the People's Republic of China* (1987), *The Philippine Bases: U.S. Security at Risk* (1987), *Crisis in the Philippines* (1984), and, with Maria Hsia Chang, *The Republic of China and U.S. Policy* (1983).

# LAND OF THE MORNING CALM
*Korea and American Security*

A. James Gregor

ETHICS AND PUBLIC POLICY CENTER

The **ETHICS AND PUBLIC POLICY CENTER,** established in 1976, conducts a program of research, writing, publications, and conferences to encourage debate on domestic and foreign policy issues among religious, educational, academic, business, political, and other leaders. A nonpartisan effort, the Center is supported by contributions (which are tax deductible) from foundations, corporations, and individuals. The authors alone are responsible for the views expressed in Center publications.

**Library of Congress Cataloging-in-Publication Data**

Gregor, A. James (Anthony James), 1929– .
Land of the morning calm : Korea and American security / A. James Gregor.
p. cm.
Includes bibliographical references.
1. United States—Foreign relations—Korea (South). 2. Korea (South)—Foreign relations—United States. 3. United States—Foreign relations—1945– .
4. Korea (South)—National security. 5. United States—National security. I. Title.
E183.8.K6G74    1989    327.7305195—dc20    89-29249 CIP

ISBN 0-89633-145-8 (alk. paper)
ISBN 0-89633-146-6 (pbk. : alk. paper)

**Distributed by arrangement with:**
University Press of America, Inc.
4720 Boston Way
Lanham, MD 20706

3 Henrietta Street
London WC2E 8LU England

All Ethics and Public Policy Center books are produced on acid-free paper. The paper used in this publication meets the minimum requirements of American National Standard for Information Sciences—Permanence of Paper for Printed Library Materials, ANSI Z39.48–1984.   ∞™

© 1990 by the Ethics and Public Policy Center. All rights reserved.
Printed in the United States of America.

**Ethics and Public Policy Center**
1030 Fifteenth Street N.W.
Washington, D.C. 20005
(202) 682-1200

*To the memory of
all those Americans and Koreans
who sacrificed their lives
in the defense of freedom*

# *Contents*

| | | |
|---|---|---|
| | Preface | ix |
| | Chronology | xiii |
| | Map | xiv |
| 1 | The Background | 1 |
| 2 | Economic Development | 19 |
| 3 | Political Development | 41 |
| 4 | External Threats | 63 |
| 5 | The Outlook | 83 |
| 6 | Implications for U.S. Policy | 105 |
| | Notes | 115 |
| | Index of Names | 125 |

# Preface

AMERICANS HAVE THE capacity to surround themselves with a cloud of comforting convictions that obscures some of the less pleasant aspects of the contemporary world. For about a decade such beliefs clouded their vision concerning the communist regime on the Chinese mainland. According to those convictions, China had transformed itself. It had abandoned Marxism-Leninism and was liberalizing. It had rejected the neo-Stalinist command economy that had wrought havoc and it had introduced capitalism. Only the horror of Tiananmen Square restored some perspective.

Similarly, most Americans have succeeded in closing their eyes to developments on the Korean peninsula. Korea and the Koreans have seemed increasingly remote. A vague sense of disquiet sometimes intrudes—when students riot or North Korean agents destroy a civilian airliner in flight. More frequently than not, however, the Korean peninsula remains at the periphery of the consciousness of Americans, even those interested in foreign affairs or the security of East Asia.

Nonetheless, significant changes have taken place on the Korean peninsula. Internal economic and political developments have transformed the Republic of Korea—the "South Korea" for which 35,000 young Americans, and countless Koreans, gave their lives not so very long ago. In the North, one of the few remaining Stalinist systems in the world continues to oppress millions—and recently the Soviet Union entered into a security relationship with the Democratic People's Republic of Korea that bodes ill.

For all the talk of lowering tensions by reducing its armed forces, Moscow has supplied the North Koreans with some of their most advanced weapon systems. For the first time since the Korean conflict in the early 1950s, the Soviet Union is providing North Korea with main battle tanks, air-superiority combat machines, and short-range missile launchers—all of which threatens the military balance on the peninsula. In exchange, the armed forces of the Soviet Union have gained access to the ports and airfields of North Korea, giving those forces a number of defensive and offensive advantages.

Potentially hostile military activity on the Korean peninsula also threatens the security of the Japanese home islands, and it increases the threat to the long sea-lanes of the Pacific. Without secure ship passage along these sea-lanes, the United States could not meet its security obligations in East Asia in the event of conflict. Sustaining forward-based military capabilities in East Asia depends on the security of the logistics connection with North America. Hostile submarines and surface raiders using facilities on the Korean peninsula could significantly increase the threat to these sea-lanes.

Indeed, the security of the Republic of Korea is a matter of general concern. Not only Japan but all of East Asia would be threatened by a major change in the military balance on the Korean peninsula. The situation in Northeast Asia is fragile, and a great deal of what will happen in Asia depends on what happens on the Korean peninsula in the not-too-distant future.

Moreover, all of East Asia is unsettled. The People's Republic of China has become increasingly menacing, not only because it has armed itself with weapon systems that threaten its neighbors, but because the violence in Tiananmen indicates that the leaders in Beijing will use whatever force they deem necessary to protect their interests, regardless of international opinion. China might very well embark on military adventures in an effort to defuse domestic tensions.

Many of the economies of the region are suffering strain as a consequence of trade friction with the United States. In the effort to accommodate Washington, for example, the Republic of Korea has allowed its national currency to appreciate against the dollar, has reduced restrictions on agricultural and industrial imports from the United States, and has voluntarily limited some exports. All these efforts have impaired the international competitiveness of South Korea's export-driven economy. That in turn has affected South Korea's internal political dynamics, which has had a negative impact on U.S.–South Korean relations and threatened the security relationship between the two countries.

The next few years will witness critical changes in Northeast Asia—and the Republic of Korea will be at the center of those changes. Indeed, developments in South Korea could very well determine the future of the region.

In the preparation of this modest work, I have become indebted to many colleagues and security professionals. Professors Jan Prybyla, John F. Copper, Byung Kyu Kang, Ki-Tak Lee, and Jong Youl Yoo provided most of the better insights found in the pages that follow. Generals Osamu Namatame and Hisatomo Matsukane and Admirals Tadashi Tajiri and Manabu Yoshida of the Japan Self-Defense Force all patiently contributed to my education. I am grateful to the Ethics and Public Policy Center for providing the support and the editorial assistance without which this work would have been impossible. Finally, to Professor Maria Hsia Chang, I am grateful for loving support and informed counsel.

# *Chronology*

| | |
|---|---|
| 1392–1910 | Yi (Chosun) Dynasty |
| 1904–1905 | Russo-Japanese War |
| 1905 | Japan establishes protectorate over Korea |
| 1910 | Japan annexes Korea |
| 1910–1945 | Occupation of Korea by Japan |
| 1945 | World War II ends—Korea divided along 38th parallel |
| 1948 | Republic of Korea established in the South and Democratic People's Republic of Korea in the North |
| 1948 | Syngman Rhee becomes president of the ROK and Kim Il-sung president of the DPRK |
| 1950–1953 | Korean War |
| 1960 | Rhee forced to resign, goes into exile |
| 1960 | Yun Po-sun becomes president of the Second Republic in the ROK |
| 1961 | Military coup in the ROK led by General Park Chung-hee |
| 1963 | Park Chung-hee becomes president of the Third Republic |
| 1972 | Joint communique on reunification signed by both North and South |
| 1972 | Under new constitution, Park becomes president of the Fourth Republic |
| 1979 | President Park assassinated |

1980      Former general Chun Doo-hwan becomes president of the Fifth Republic

1988      Roh Tae-woo becomes president of the Sixth Republic

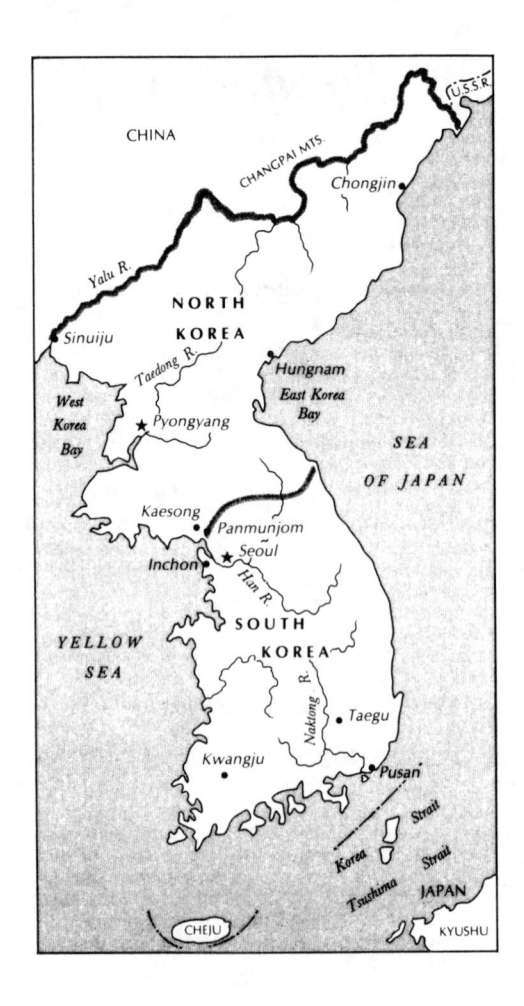

From *The New Columbia Encyclopedia* (copyright © 1975, Columbia University Press). Used by permission.

# 1
# *The Background*

KOREA HAS BEEN an identifiable historical, cultural, and political presence in East Asia for millennia. More than two thousand years before the common era, the Tung-i or "Eastern barbarian bowmen" occupied what we now identify as the "land of the morning calm," bringing an Altaic language, rice cultivation, a matrilineal family system, and a collection of political myths with them. By the beginning of the common era, the tribal leagues that had settled on the peninsula, already identified as Chosun (or Choson) by Chinese scholars, began to coalesce into politically integrated communities. By the fifth century, three states—Koguryo in the north, Silla in the south along the Han River, and Paekche in the far south at the foot of the peninsula—had each developed a working state structure informed by Confucian and Buddhist convictions and governed by heredity monarchs.

Over the next several centuries the states of the Korean peninsula expanded and contracted with the ebb and flow of Chinese and Mongol aggression. At times one state would ally itself with external powers to defeat its neighbors, and at other times the several states would unite in a collaborative effort. In the eighth century, Silla became a sovereign political community extending over almost the entire Korean peninsula. It incorporated within its confines the majority of people in Koguryo and Paekche.

Internal strife undermined and ultimately destroyed the high civilization of Silla. Upon its ruins, Koryo, a centralized monarchy, was established in the tenth century, but it was despoiled and its territory occupied by Mongol invaders in 1238. Along the coasts, Japanese pirates launched military operations that threatened the integrity of the entire peninsula. Finally, Korean General Yi Song-gye mobilized resistance against the external aggressors. Strengthened by internal political and economic reform, the new dynasty founded by Yi—officially designated Chosun—became one of the longest continuous regimes in political history. Established in 1392, the Yi (Chosun) Dynasty lasted until 1910, ending only after Korea had been fatally weakened in an unequal contest with the rising industrialized countries of the West.[1]

One fact immediately stands out from this cursory review of Korea's history: the peninsula has been regularly subject to incursions from predatory neighbors. The Korean peninsula is at a strategic intersection in East Asia, located at a juncture where the interests of major powers have converged since prehistoric times. As a result, political and military violence has played a major role in shaping the psychology and culture of modern Koreans.[2]

*Land, People, and Policy*

Korea is a peninsula extending southward about 700 miles from the East Asian mainland. It separates the Yellow Sea from the Sea of Japan. The peninsula and its associated islands fall between 124 degrees and 132 degrees east latitude and 33 degrees and 43 degrees north longitude. Korea shares a 500-mile-long land boundary with China, and throughout its pre-modern history was open to incursions from the nomadic horsemen of Siberia and Mongolia. Its eastern coast faces Japan, and the Japanese have used the peninsula as a stepping-stone to the mainland.

The peninsula covers about 86,000 square miles, roughly the size of Pennsylvania. Its present population is some 63 million; about 21 million are in the North as citizens of the Democratic People's Republic of Korea (DPRK), and over 42 million are in the South as citizens of the Republic of Korea (ROK).

The present division of Korea into two sovereign and competitive states attests to its strategic position. By the beginning of the 1950s, both the industrialized democracies and the emerging Soviet bloc sought to dominate the peninsula because of its military importance vis-a-vis the Asian continent. The Soviets clearly understood that armed forces on the Korean peninsula would enjoy strategic advantages in any conflict with Japan. The peninsula, by serving as a staging area for hostile forces, would constitute a dagger pointed at the Japanese home islands. The flight time from Korea to the major Japanese urban areas and their support infrastructures could be measured in minutes. Naval bases on the coast of the peninsula could interdict sea traffic through the choke points at the Korean straits.[3]

Conversely, the industrialized democracies understood that armed forces on the peninsula would give them access to the invasion routes into the Soviet maritime provinces in the Siberian East and into the major industrial centers of communist China in Manchuria.

Since time immemorial, invaders have traveled over the corridors of the Korean peninsula, and major naval engagements in the surrounding waters have shaped the destiny of Asia. At the conclusion of World War II, the people of Korea were once again embroiled in a conflict between competing foreign interests. Although U.S. policy was generally confused, it was clearly committed to rapid disengagement on the Korean peninsula. U.S. policy had been influenced by a number of curious assessments, including the belief that Mao Zedong and his "agrarian reformers" would not make common cause with the Soviet Union. Thus by 1949, the United States had withdrawn its troops from Korea.

The invasion of the ROK by the armed forces of the DPRK on June 25, 1950, resulted from several factors, but the U.S. decision to reduce its obligations in Korea and withdraw its troops obviously contributed to the North Korean decision to unify the nation by force.

The invasion of South Korea compelled a reconsideration of U.S. policy. The invasion seemed to have at least the tacit support of the Soviet Union. Coupled with the fact that two days before North Korean troops crossed the 38th parallel, Mao Zedong announced unequivocally that China would unite "firmly . . . with the Soviet Union" in its revolutionary initiatives in Asia,[4] this apparent Soviet support gave the invasion every appearance of being a concerted and calculated attack upon the interests of the Western industrial democracies. It was clear that Japan, South Korea, and the remnants of the Nationalist Republic of China on Taiwan would be defenseless in the face of such an onslaught without the intervention of U.S. armed forces.

Suddenly, all the subtle qualifications that had influenced U.S. policy in Asia rang false. Once again, the thinking that had informed U.S. opinion in the earlier part of the twentieth century became relevant. East Asia loomed large as a place where long-term U.S. interests might be compromised by flawed policy. Unless the United States was prepared to withdraw from all of East Asia, Washington would have to intervene in any armed conflict on the peninsula to prevent the Soviet Union and its allies from dominating all of Korea—and thereby threatening all of Asia.

As early as the first years of the century, Alfred Thayer Mahan, the geostrategist and advocate of naval power, had argued that Asia would become critical to the future of the United States and the West. He maintained that the vast populations involved and the economic and commercial potential would render the entire region of paramount importance to the "progress of civilization."[5]

To foster that progress, and to protect their interests, the Western powers, which are separated from East Asia by vast oceanic distances, would have to depend on sea power and access to facilities in the region to offset the advantages of the expanding land-based Russian power that looked to its own "national and racial" interests in East Asia. Mahan's analysis was remarkable prescient. He anticipated that Japan, however aggressively it pursued its own interests, could not long sustain activities on the Asian continent. In his judgment, the Western powers, together with local forces, would ultimately have to "contain" not Japan, but Russia, denying it free access to the open Pacific and the critical sea-lanes of communication in the region.

Mahan emphasized the importance of the Korean peninsula, not only as a land bridge to the Asian continent, but as a source of critical choke points affecting the flow of sea traffic to all of Northeast Asia. In effect, half a century before the North Koreans invaded the South, long before the advent of the Cold War and the policy recommendations associated with George Kennan, Admiral Mahan advanced a rationale for an anti-Soviet containment policy.[6]

The invasion of the ROK by the communist forces from the DPRK served as a catalyst; it transformed U.S. strategic thinking in East Asia, and underlined the importance of the Korean peninsula to regional security. Once again Korea's geography influenced its relations with surrounding states. More than ten thousand miles of exposed coastline—and territorial waters dotted with another three thousand miles of exposed coastline—suddenly were recognized as strategically important by the major powers. Once again, the narrows of the Korean straits were perceived as affording egress to the open Pacific for Soviet vessels otherwise confined to the inland waters of the Sea of Japan. Once again, the T'aebaeksan Mountains that run north-south along the peninsula were seen as providing the invasion corridor down which hostile forces would almost certainly travel.

The Korean conflict that began in 1950 and ended with the armistice of 1953 cost the United States 34,000 killed and over 100,000 wounded. Almost four million Koreans lost their lives in the struggle. Hundreds of thousands of Korean women were widowed and hundreds of thousands of Korean children were orphaned. About 120,000 South Koreans were executed by the invaders from the North on the pretext that they were "reactionaries," "running dogs of capitalism," and "counter-revolutionaries."[7] Korea's cities were devastated. Seoul, the capital of the Republic of Korea, changed hands four times in the three years of conflict and by 1953 was reduced to rubble.

Korea had once again assumed its historical function as a pawn in the strategic calculations of external powers. As in prehistoric times, the armed invaders of the twentieth century destroyed settlements and rendered the land unproductive. In fact, the peninsula has enjoyed little respite throughout this century. In the years between the two world wars, Korean guerrilla bands supported by the Soviet Union often engaged Japanese forces.

Korea has in effect been a prisoner of its geography throughout its history. Whatever the cultural advantages that came over the invasion routes, they were purchased at a high price by the Korean people.

## *Reform in the Nineteenth and Twentieth Centuries*

With the advent of the nineteenth century, Korea's ruling elite realized that the nation required massive reform if it were to survive in an increasingly hazardous world. European ideas had begun to circulate among the more sophisticated Koreans, and European commercial competition had begun to threaten the integrity of the Korean domestic economy. The British had undertaken their first voyages in the early years of the century, and by 1840 both the Russians and the French had won cooperation from Korean merchants.

By mid-nineteenth century, all of Korea was in ferment. New patterns of commercial relations, altered currency flows, new religious ideas, and significant changes in the distribution of political power and personal wealth all contributed to widespread social tension. Peasant wars exacerbated the problems produced by the first European contacts. The response to these external influences was one that was to become common throughout mainland Asia. Some advocated the complete and immediate repulsion of foreign commercial and intellectual influence while others called for selective adoption and adaptation of European practices and ideas to render Korea more capable of competing in the modern world.

By the last quarter of the nineteenth century, Korea had fewer and fewer options. In 1876, with the Treaty of Kanghwa, Korea was finally formally opened to the West. Commercial treaties were signed with the United States, France, Great Britain, Germany, and Russia. In the ensuing competition, pressure from Japan mounted, and in response the Korean monarchy sought the active assistance of Imperial China. At almost the same time, Russia attempted to extend its influence by drawing Korea into a secret security arrangement. The British, in an effort to offset the initiatives of the Czar, occupied the Korean port of Komundo in 1885; they withdrew only after Russia pledged to make no further inroads in Korea.

A decade later, however, the Russians regained the initiative by expelling Japanese advisers in Seoul and forcing Korea to accept Russian economic penetration in the northern reaches of the nation. The Russo-Japanese rivalry was temporarily stabilized in the Rosen/Nishi Convention of 1898, in which both sides pledged to protect the national independence of Korea. Spheres of influence were carved out on the peninsula, and the Japanese, foreshadowing later events, proposed a division of the Korean nation along the 38th parallel.

All of this competition among foreigners for control of Korea gave rise to episodic violence. Indigenous forces mounted rebellions in an effort to reorganize and strengthen the nation, and external predators sought advantage in the general confusion. Like most of the nations of Asia, Korea was unstable. In response, a number of individuals and groups advocated thoroughgoing reform of the prevailing political and economic system to defend against foreign incursions. Even the political elite of the Yi Dynasty attempted a vigorous reform campaign in the early 1880s to emulate the modernization movement of Meiji Japan. That ineffectual initiative was followed by an American-inspired reform movement advocated by the Indepedence Society.

The society, through its bilingual newspaper *Tongnip Sinmun,* advocated the introduction of Western reforms, including the expansion of educational opportunity; the guarantee of citizen rights; the construction of a more adequate communication, transportation, and financial infrastructure; and the establishment of a representative national assembly. The Independence Society sought the economic development and political modernization of Korea in a frantic effort to forestall the loss of its sovereign independence.[8]

However serious and well intentioned, the Korean reform movements proved to be far too little and too late. The Anglo-

Japanese treaty of alliance in 1902 gave Japan international recognition of its claims to the Korean peninsula. In its effort to contain Russian expansion, Great Britain was prepared to support Japan's intrusions in Korea.

Two years later, Japan and Russia engaged in a war that ended in the destruction of the Russian fleet and the defeat of its attempts to dominate Korea and Manchuria. During the conflict, the Japanese occupied Seoul, and in February 1904 they compelled the Korean government to sign a protocol that permitted Japan to station troops on Korean soil and effectively control Korean life.

By the time of the Portsmouth Peace Conference of 1905, Korea was "placed at Japan's free disposal," the systematic Japanese colonization of the peninsula was formally undertaken, and Great Britain and the United States acknowledged Japan's primacy in Korea.[9]

Korea, it was now clear, could not maintain its sovereign independence without internal political strength and economic viability. Throughout its history, Korea had had to undertake cooperative security arrangements with external powers. The circumstances were influenced by the ability of Korea's political leadership to negotiate from strength, which required not only political unity, but economic capacity. The political reformers and economic revolutionaries in the latter part of the nineteenth century understood this and advocated strategies to produce both. Their failure was the failure of the system. On August 22, 1910, Japan annexed Korea.

Korea had failed to meet the challenges of the late nineteenth century. It could reform neither its politics nor its economic system to meet prevailing circumstances. It required a rapid expansion of its economic capabilities to sustain a stable political order and provide the underpinning for a defense against potential aggressors. Korea's problems had become apparent to its patriots. What was not clear was how to resolve them.

By the time Korea had opened to the influence of the West, it was dangerously late. Japan had mastered the rudiments of economic development and industrialization, while Korea was ruled by a monarchical system virtually devoid of economic and intellectual resources.

In many ways, Korea in the nineteenth century was remarkably retrograde. Slavery persisted in many parts of the kingdom. The monarchy had difficulty extracting revenue from the population. Of all the taxes collected, only 20 or 30 percent ever found their way to Seoul. The nation had no effective banking system, and the bureaucracy, though well schooled in conservative Confucian exegesis, was all but totally ignorant of the potential for social change implicit in the economic and political influences emanating from the West.

This is not at all surprising. One of the major tasks of the twentieth century has been to define and alleviate the nature and causes of economic and political retardation. For more than half the century, it can be argued, intellectuals in both the advanced the less-developed countries have failed to discharge their responsibilities. Only recently has the nature of the problem and the strategy for its redress become reasonably apparent. It is not surprising that the Koreans at the turn of the century failed fully to anticipate that strategy. What *is* surprising is that Western intellectuals have only recently begun to identify and understand its elements.

*Development and Modernization Strategies*

The problems that afflicted Korea at the end of the nineteenth century were common to many political communities. The nations that had already undergone some measure of economic development and industrialization were largely restricted to Western Europe and North America. Eastern and Southern Europe, although quickening their economic activity, lagged behind Britain, Germany, and France. By the end of the nineteenth century, Imperial Russia and monarchical Italy had begun their economic expansion. Asia, with the notable exception of Meiji Japan, remained backward. Latin America had hardly begun to emerge from traditional agricultural pursuits, and Africa languished far behind the rest.

By the end of World War I, developments in Eastern and Southern Europe captured the imagination of Western intellectuals. By some curious alchemy, the Marxism of the nineteenth century was transformed from a social and political ideology into an ideology of economic development and industrialization. The Bolsheviks seized power not because they could marshall the "vast majority" of the oppressed proletariat, but because they succeeded in enlisting military deserters and displaced peasants, who were concentrated in the urban centers of Russia devastated by World War I. By the time of Lenin's death, it was evident that what Bolshevik Russia required was not social experiment, but rapid industrialization.

Heavy industry was largely devoted to providing weapon systems to protect the new Soviet state from internal rebellion and external threat. Stalinism was a response to a real or fancied external threat; it was nationalistic in appeal. Many supported Stalinism, not because they saw in its features a transmogrified Marxism, but because they were nationalists and sought to ensure the continuity of "Mother Russia."

None of this was lost on the revolutionaries of the East. Mao Zedong from his earliest youth conceived of Marxism, in its Bolshevik variant, as an ideology of redemption for a China that was prey to "imperialist" forces. Chinese communism became little more than nationalist affirmation and a program for rapid economic development. Very few of the Chinese founders of Marxism knew anything of classical Marxism. What appealed to them was the Marxism that had been transformed by the heavy hand of Stalin.

In substance, between the two world wars, and certainly after the second, many revolutionaries in less-developed countries viewed Marxism as a means of achieving national independence and the rapid economic development of their respective communities.

It is against that background that the political aspirations and revolutionary activities of North Korea's Kim Il-sung are best understood. Kim Il-sung, "the most outstanding Marxist-Leninist, with whom no other leader of any country can compare," became a "socialist" because he believed Marxism could best defeat Japan's imperialism.[10] With his accession to power at the end of World War II, he advocated *juche,* a developmental program predicated on unalloyed Stalinism, that is, a self-reliant form of economic development.

Inspired by the Soviet example, Kim Il-sung established a centralized political system to manage the population. The Korean communist party, officially known as the Korean Workers' Party, would be animated by a "unitary ideological system," and would establish "rigid discipline" in which all Koreans would "breathe in the same way, talk in the same way, and act unitedly."[11] Kim Il-sung also aligned North Korea with what used to be the Communist Internationale—with the Soviet Union and the People's Republic of China (PRC) to defend itself from the putative depredations of "international capitalism."

The leaders of North Korea believed that such support was necessary but not sufficient to defend national sovereignty. Circumstances required that this support be coupled with rapid economic development. Kim Il-sung sought that development by imposing Stalinist discipline on his people. To this day, all the major attributes of Stalinism characterize the political system of North Korea: the hysterical adulation of the "greatest man of our times, one of the greatest men in modern history, the outstanding leader of the revolution"; the establishment of a totalitarian party; the imposition of bureaucratic control of the economy; the construction of a vast military machine; and the inflexible control of information, education, and the personal behavior of all segments of the population.

For years after the end of World War II, this near-total control was the model for revolutionaries throughout the world. Revolutionaries in less-developed countries touted the Soviet Union as the prime example of anti-imperialist and developmental success.[12] The Soviet Union after all had not only withstood imperialist aggression, but had emerged from World War II as a major military power. It had demonstrated that state planning could accelerate economic growth and foster rapid industrialization.[13] Kim Il-sung responded to this vision of Stalinism, which seemed to provide answers to problems that had afflicted Korea throughout the nineteenth and twentieth centuries and to address other concerns that were as old as the nation itself.

The division of Korea along the 38th parallel isolated Kim Il-sung's revolution in the North. In the South, the United States sponsored the creation of an alternative Korea, the Republic of Korea. Addressing the same problems faced by Kim Il-sung, the leaders of the South sought to formulate their own developmental strategy, not only to foster economic and industrial development, but to establish fully ROK's sovereign integrity.

Among the many difficulties faced by the leaders of the ROK was their lack of a preconceived "plan" to tackle their arduous responsibilities. They were looked upon skeptically by some Western intellectuals who believed that "the establishment of a socialist planned economy" was an essential, indeed indispensable, condition for the attainment of economic and social progress in underdeveloped countries.[14] Even non-Marxist Westerners were arguing that "an underdeveloped country should have . . . an overall integrated national plan" to stimulate economic growth and self-sustained industrialization. There was talk of the need of "superplanning" to achieve significant results.[15] Ultimately, even the anti-socialists contended that government in less-developed countries would have to assume many obligations, including taking on "essential, major technical tasks," mobilizing resources to construct an elaborate communications and transportation infrastructure, and paying the social costs of accelerated development.[16]

Those charged with governing the new republic in the South were not at all clear what course they should follow. The most active political elements opposed Marxist-Leninism in whatever guise. And the association with the United States—despite some American academics' enthusiasm for planning—was a force supporting a market-governed system. Furthermore, the Allied occupation forces that moved in after the surrender of the Japanese in 1945 brought in Western notions about economics. Like most educated Americans, the members of the U.S. military government were economic traditionalists. They believed that "profit maximization" provided the motive for enterprise, and that the purpose of government, by and large, was to ensure "freedom for all commerical transactions."[17]

The Korean leaders were also familiar with the Japanese example of rapid growth and industrialization. The annual average rate of economic growth in pre-war Japan, from 1900 to 1940, had been about 4 percent—high compared with other economies.[18] While no two instances of sustained development are identical, most Asians looked to the Japanese accomplishment as a model.

Most Asians, and Koreans in particular, recognized that modernization required a revolutionary change in the political and social structure. It was the Meiji Restoration in Japan that transformed an essentially traditional society into a dynamic, self-sustained one of rapid growth and industrialization. During the Restoration, the government asserted its authority throughout the nation. Young Japanese were sent abroad to study Western science and technology. Foreigners were invited to Japan to teach management skills and techniques. The government provided the capital for new industries. And the longstanding tradition of collective discipline and teamwork contributed to the rapid growth and capital accumulation.

The economic development of Japan, and the revolutionary social and political changes, were undertaken by an elite committed to protecting their country from external threat. They understood that the necessary changes could not be allowed to destabilize the political system, for that would render the nation vulnerable. As a consequence, the vast structural changes that characterized the Meiji Restoration were undertaken without destroying the prevailing social and political system.

Out of these conflicting ideas and forces, the leadership of the ROK would have to put together an economic program. The program would have to be one that allowed market mechanisms to operate. Yet it would have to cede a major role to politics, since national leaders would be responsible for seeing that the best use was made of available resources. In effect, the growth program of the ROK would be in the hands of a political leadership committed to making sure that market mechanisms initiate and sustain an escalating rate of economic expansion. Economic activity, that is, would be neither laissez-faire nor planned, but "mixed" in character.

Unlike the DPRK, with its well-articulated economic policy,

the ROK would face a long period of trial and error before it settled on a national program of growth and modernization.

*First Years of Korean Independence*

The establishment of the Republic of Korea resulted from the inability of the major powers at the close of World War II to agree on the character of the political community that was to emerge. For the Soviet Union, an anti-Soviet regime in Korea was unthinkable. For the United States, a Soviet-dominated Korea would betray the interests of the Western democracies. The inescapable result was the creation of two Koreas, the Marxist-Leninist Korea of Kim Il-sung in the North, and the non-socialist Korea of Syngman Rhee (Yi Sung-man) in the South.

Whatever else he was, Syngman Rhee was a consummate politician with a long history of devotion to Korean independence. On his return to Korea after the Japanese surrender he threw himself indefatigably into political activity (undeterred by the fact that the U.S. military government found him headstrong and abrasive). By the time of the United Nations–sponsored elections of May 1948, Rhee had become indispensable to U.S. hopes of stabilizing Korea south of the 38th parallel. On August 15, 1948, government authority was transferred from the U.S. military forces to the newly established Republic of Korea under the presidency of Syngman Rhee. At almost the same time, Kim Il-sung was declared premier of the Democratic People's Republic of Korea. The division of the Korean peninsula was institutionalized.

For the first few years, most of the political energy of the two Koreas was consumed in stabilizing their respective systems. The regime in the North broke the back of any resistance by purging the system of "traitors, collaborators, oppressors of the working classes, lackies of world imperialism, and reactionaries." As early as 1949 about 90 percent of all industrial production and more than half of trade and sales were in the hands of the state bureaucracy, and private property and entrepreneurship had ceased to exist. The Soviet Union supplied economic assistance that favored heavy industry.[19]

At the same time, the DPRK organized campaigns against "familialism" to alter the traditional behavior that prevented the individual and the family from identifying fully with the new Marxist state.[20] The Korean Workers' Party sought to assume the role of the family and to create the emotional attachment that had traditionally been reserved for filial and familial relations. In June 1949, Kim Il-sung became chairman of the Korean Workers' Party and consolidated his hold over both the party and the state. Possessed of personal power and assured of Soviet support, Kim proceeded to infiltrate agents into the ROK, hoping to destabilize the fragile system that was emerging.

Although Rhee had been elected president by an overwhelming vote of the ROK National Assembly, the assembly immediately attempted to weaken his personal power. In response, Rhee introduced a land reform bill in February 1950 to undermine the political influence of landlords, who preferred an executive too weak to work against their interests.

Rhee was also forced to contend with an armed insurrection of indigenous communists, supported by the communist regime in the DPRK. In 1950 the uprising was suppressed, but at the cost of many lives and systematic repression.[21]

All this activity in the two Koreas left little energy for economic development. By the outbreak of the Korean War both states were still attempting to solidify their regimes.

In June 1950, with the apparent concurrence of Joseph Stalin and Mao Zedong, Kim Il-sung launched an armed invasion of the South. In the three years of that war, both parts of the peninsula were devastated. In the ROK, almost half the industrial assets suffered substantial damage; in Seoul itself, over 80 percent of the industry, public utilities, and transport, 75 percent of the office buildings, and 50 percent of the private dwellings lay in ruins. Much of the physical capital inherited from the Japanese colonial regime was dissipated.

The communist regime in the DPRK fared no better. Kim Il-sung, however, had the advantage of a developmental program that had long since been standardized in the Soviet Union and was being implemented in the PRC. In the three-year plan that commenced in 1954, Kim gave paramount priority to the development of heavy industry at the cost of light industry and agriculture.[22]

In the ROK, there was no clear economic policy and economic decisions were influenced by distinct constituencies in very different ways. Circumstances required the reconstruction of the industrial facilities and the communications infrastructure, but no other consistent tactics were pursued. The economy was wracked by a high rate of inflation that ranged between 25 and 80 percent. This situation was worsened by a confusing system of multiple exchange rates that tended to discourage exports and encourage imports. The result was increasing national indebtedness.

To offset these tendencies, a complicated system of import and export licensing was introduced. Only certain items were eligible for import, and those items were subject to tariff rates varying from zero to more than 100 percent, and averaging about 40 percent.

To counteract the export disincentives created by the overvalued *won* (the Korean monetary unit), the government established a foreign exchange system that allowed export earnings to be used to purchase popular and profitable imports. As an added incentive, exporters were given direct subsidies and concessional loans at lower than prevailing rates.

The incentives to export produced only marginal results. The basic policy was a form of import substitution in which local manufacturers were protected by high tariffs on competitive imports. The entire system was supported by substantial U.S. aid in the form of grants. By 1960 about 87 percent of all ROK imports were financed by U.S. funding. Between 1953 and 1960 about 10 percent of the ROK gross national product (GNP) was provided by U.S. economic assistance funds. U.S. grant aid and concessional loans accounted for nearly half of the nation's savings and investment and generated more than half the government's revenues.[23]

The failure of the ROK to pursue a coherent policy of growth and development was reflected in the economic conditions in the years following the war. In the rural countryside, some peasants lived at the very margin of subsistence. University graduates went directly into the unemployment lines. In the early 1960s, the industrial system exported goods worth about $2 per capita annually, and imported ten times as much. Of a per capita GNP of about $80, 1.6 percent was devoted to domestic savings at a time when it was estimated that a domestic savings rate of about 10 percent of GNP would be required to fund self-sustained economic growth. Fully 80 percent of the nation's GNP was consumed as subsistence while only 12 percent went into investment.[24]

In sum, the Republic of Korea gave every evidence of economic stagnation. Factoring in the ROK's rate of population growth, the per capita GNP of the South grew at an annual real rate of only 1.7 percent in the early 1960s. What seemed to be emerging was a growth-impaired system irremediably dependent on U.S. aid.

In the DPRK, on the other hand, the situation appeared dramatically different. If we use 1955 as an index (1955 = 100), manufacturing output escalated from 61 in 1954 to 212 in 1958; available electric energy rose from 63 in 1954 to 235 in 1958; and overall productivity climbed from 67 in 1954 to 217 in 1958. The Five Year Plan that followed continued the pace of development.

Between 1954 and 1960, the number of DPRK industrial workers almost doubled: from 21 percent of the work force to 38.3 percent. Of course, the entire process of industrialization was reinforced by substantial foreign aid from the Soviet Union and the PRC.

Kim Il-sung had by now become undisputed leader of the DPRK. Under his dominance, the Korean Workers' Party created a network of organizations into which the entire labor force was mobilized. All industry had been nationalized and all agricultural land had been collectivized. As a consequence, a thoroughly domesticated labor force was marshalled, and it was continually exhorted to exceed state-mandated quotas. The result was high productivity at controlled wages, with the difference between output and wages accruing to the state as capital surplus.

The narrow base from which growth began, the large amounts of foreign aid, the docile work force, and the responsiveness of a relatively simple economy to central planning produced a rate of industrial growth in the DPRK that averaged 34 percent per annum from 1956 through 1960. By the beginning of the 1960s, it appeared that the DPRK would overwhelm the ROK. The DPRK economy seemed able to sustain a growing military potential that would soon threaten the very survival of the non-socialist regime in the South. The ROK was politically unstable, its economy was fragile, its dependence on the United States was abject, and its defense capabilities were inadequate. In 1963 Scandinavia's leading commercial newspaper prophesied that the ROK had no future.

# 2
# *Economic Development*

BY THE EARLY 1960s, the Democratic People's Republic of Korea in the North conceived of itself as a model for less-developed nations aspiring to modernization, a "rich textbook for people in the countries . . . fighting for economic independence." In the judgment of Pyongyang's admirers, "Comrade Kim Il-sung, with his scientific policy and his extraordinary revolutionary sweep, has led the party and the people successfully to the construction of an independent national economy by the shortest possible route." The Marxist-Leninists of the DPRK argued that "it is wholly because of the guidance of the genius of Comrade Kim Il-sung that the once extremely backward Korean people were able to win through thick and thin . . . and enjoy the great national prosperity unprecedented in the history of the fatherland." Kim's developmental program had created a "magnificent socialist paradise in the northern half of the republic," while "South Korea's industry had been subjugated to foreign capital; its agriculture had been ruined; [and its] economy had become an economy of flowing tears in which bankruptcy and starvation bloom."[1]

Through the last years of the 1950s and into the early 1960s the economy of North Korea did experience substantial growth. In 1959, the leadership in the DPRK conjured up the "Chollima movement," emulating Mao's "Great Leap Forward," in which the labor force was exhorted to surpass goals and to work ceaselessly and selflessly for non-material rewards in the service of socialism. Exemplary workers and outstanding production units were rewarded with Chollima titles. The regime claimed that the movement generated enthusiasm, increased productivity, and encouraged innovation and creativity.

In the ROK, on the other hand, economic expansion and development were negligible throughout the 1950s. By 1959, the annual real rate of economic growth in the South was about 2 percent, barely enough to exceed the increase in population. U.S. grant aid and concessional assistance supplied the difference between the relatively low rate of real growth and no growth at all. Without it, "the economic condition of the population would have remained desperate."[2] If the main challenge of the twentieth century was to develop and expand backward economies, the experience on the Korean peninsula seemed to recommend the regime in the North as a model rather than the regime in the South.

But the process of development had only begun. The most crucial phases of growth, technological change, and structural transformation would occur in the next quarter of a century, a period that would shape the present and have a great impact on the future.

*Democratic People's Republic of Korea*

The economic development of the DPRK was favored by a number of factors. Most of the peninsula's raw materials, including anthracite coal, lignite, iron ore, and nonferrous metals, were located in the North. The DPRK had about half the population of the ROK, and approximately the same amount of arable land, if a somewhat harsher climate and a shorter growing season. Beyond that, most of the development sponsored by the Japanese had taken place in the North, and about 90 percent of Korea's total energy-generating capacity was located there. Although much was destroyed during the Korean conflict, a nucleus remained around which new industries developed. Finally, the regime of Kim Il-sung received massive economic and technical assistance from both the Soviet Union and the PRC, about the same amount per capita as was received by the ROK.[3] These advantages helped but they do not totally explain the differences in performance between the DPRK and ROK.

The advantages, together with enthusiasm, a firm commitment

to a neo-Stalinist developmental strategy, a relatively simple economy, and a compliant labor force, produced an impressive rate of real growth in North Korea for about a decade between 1953 and the first years of the 1960s, when almost 40 percent of the work force was employed in industrial production—up from the 20 percent at the end of the Korean War.

In retrospect, these accomplishments contained the germ of failure. Like the Soviet Union and the PRC, the DPRK had relentlessly created heavy industries and machine tool factories to the neglect of the agricultural sector; external trade was conducted almost exclusively with socialist states and was characterized by an exchange of products that were singularly noncompetitive on world markets; and the population received only rationed necessities. Stable but low wages allowed the government to accumulate resources for massive capital investments. The systematic exploitation of labor, however, impaired the motivation to increase productivity.

The developmental "socialism" identified with Stalinism—and pursued in North Korea—assigns primacy to heavy industry and machine tool factories. Heavy industry is necessary to develop military strength to protect the revolutionary state against the threat of capitalist aggression. Hence, Kim Il-sung insisted that "heavy industry constitutes the material basis for the country's political and economic independence."[4]

Beyond that, the emphasis on heavy industry typifies centrally planned economies. Large sums, extracted from a largely passive population, are available to the leaders who seek a rapid increase in the gross value of output. Massive projects of high visibility produce impressive statistics. Because such systems do not have to respond to non-governmental demand, they do not have to produce marketable products or satisfy quality and demand criteria.

In market systems, allocative decisions are made through hundreds and thousands of transactions in which individuals try to calculate investment profitability. In centrally planned systems, decisions are made by bureaucratic committees more concerned with statistical yield than with efficiency or serviceability of product. Bureaucrats, plant managers, floor supervisors, and individual workers are rewarded for filling and surpassing production quotas. Growth is generated by infusions of capital and labor, both under state control. But innovation and enterprise cannot be controlled by the state. Throughout the Marxist-Leninist world, increments in gross output are accompanied by remarkably little technological improvement, enhanced labor productivity, or quality control.

In such a system, because there are typically no utility costs involved in the use of resources, there is a tendency to overcapitalize. The disposition is to expand but also to hoard resources to meet future state quotas that may be unreasonable. The heavy industries produce the requisites for the capital goods industries that contribute to the institutional goals of the planning bureaucracies. The entire process is unconstrained by objective economic considerations such as opportunity costs, resource scarcities, or factor endowments, unlike in market-governed systems, where utility and profitability ultimately constrain investment and influence production schedules.

That first period of industrial development, however, must ultimately mature into one of balanced growth. At some point, production for production's sake must generate goods for end-users. Weapon systems must work and machine tools must function properly.

In Marxist-Leninist economies, the ordinary consumers are generally ill-served. Their needs are rarely considered by the planning community. But even if consumer needs are ignored, capital goods—tools, instruments, processed materials, plants—must be serviceable if further production schedules are to be met. However, the character of the system, whatever the advertised rate of growth, makes it increasingly difficult to meet the test of serviceability. Light industry is neglected, inventories accumulate, redundancy and waste abound. In the final analysis, the consuming public absorbs the inefficiencies and shortfalls—housing, agricultural products, roads, railroads, schools, hospitals, retail outlets, service centers are all in short supply.

As a consequence, these "command" economies go through periodic "reform," "restructuring," and "liberalization." In this regard, the leadership of communist China has been perhaps the most candid. In the post-Maoist period, PRC economists have identified the disabilities of the economic growth strategy pursued for almost three decades under Mao Zedong. They have catalogued a list of systemic weaknesses in the communist Chinese economy that includes an overall decline in the productivity of both capital and labor, a scandalous overinvestment in redundant and non-productive industrial assets, and the stockpiling in inventory of useless products and defective goods, all at the expense of the nation's standard of living.[5] Almost all the Marxist-Leninist economies—Cuba, Hungary, Vietnam, the USSR—have revealed the same disabilities.

By the mid-1960s, the DPRK economy was beginning to have identical problems. After 1966, the North Korean authorities no longer published data on grain production, suggesting that yields were declining as a result of the low investment rates in agriculture. It appeared that North Korea could meet the basic food needs of the population only through strict rationing.

In 1964, only 20 percent of total state investment was allocated to agriculture, while 60 percent was earmarked for heavy industry.[6] (And that 20 percent was the highest proportion in the history of the DPRK.)

The consequences were predictable. The production goals of the Seven Year Plan, to be fulfilled by 1967, were not attained; the plan was extended to 1970 and still not fulfilled.

Finally, even the analysts in Pyongyang attributed the failures to hypercentralization, a command economy, "formalism," and "bureaucratism," which generally translate into misallocation of resources, general inefficiency, and imbalances in output.[7] These disabilities were aggravated by the partial withdrawal of Soviet aid.

The unwillingness of the DPRK to take sides in the Sino-Soviet conflict, and Soviet-DPRK disagreements over economic plans, led to a substantial reduction in Soviet aid by the mid-1960s. The result was the failure of several major projects, including an oil refinery, several power plants, and some metallurgical combines. All this seriously compromised the economic prospects of the DPRK. In 1970, the Pyongyang leadership decided to modify the development strategy that had guided the nation's economy since 1948 by importing machinery and even whole plants from the capitalist countries, primarily Japan and the Western European nations. By 1974, 60 percent of DPRK imports were from non-socialist sources, as contrasted to 11 percent in 1971.

The decision made at least two things evident: (1) the socialist nations could not, or would not, make advanced technology available to kindred states; and (2) DPRK products were not competitive on the world market.

What was largely conjecture in 1970 has since been fully confirmed. Except in selected areas of specialization—almost exclusively in the field of weapon systems—the socialist economies lag far behind the market economies in terms of quality, technological sophistication, and innovation. Since that time, almost every socialist economy has sought technology transfers from the non-socialist market systems.

The DPRK entered the 1980s with a laggard economy barely capable of providing minimum health, education, housing, and subsistence for its population. Management and production skills are increasingly being sought outside the circle of socialist states. Regulations allowing foreign companies to enter into joint ventures in North Korea were promulgated in 1984. To date, however, there has been a disappointing response. The cumbersome and unresponsive bureaucratic system has made North Korea unattractive.

Some marginal experiments in liberalization and reform have been undertaken with the establishment of a network of "direct sales stores" (about two hundred throughout the entire country) to stimulate competition among producers and improve the quality and assortment of consumer goods. So far, however, these experiments have had little effect.

The productive system of North Korea is encumbered, moreover, by policy imperatives that allocate as much as 20 percent of the GNP to the military. Burdened by these demands, and freighted with the intrinsic difficulties of neo-Stalinist economic policies, the DPRK has fallen behind the rest of East Asia.

Although it is difficult to compare economic systems, the per capita national income in communist Korea is probably less than

$1,000, making it one of the lowest among the developing countries in the region. By 1985, the per capita national income was more than thirteen times higher in Singapore, six times higher in Hong Kong, five times higher in Taiwan, and twice as high in the Republic of Korea. By the mid-1980s, it appeared that South Korea had won the economic race with the North and that the differences between the two would probably increase rather than diminish in the future.

## Republic of Korea: Land Reform

The remarkable economic development of the Republic of Korea could not be foreseen in the early 1960s. Under the leadership of Syngman Rhee, the ROK had chosen policies that were not well articulated, well planned, or well implemented. The combination of an overvalued currency and high tariffs discouraged foreign investment, insulated domestic producers from foreign competition, diminished export potential, and made the nation dependent on foreign aid.

The domestic system of controlled access to foreign exchange imposed by the Rhee administration contributed to widespread corruption among government officials. The entrepreneurial and propertied classes, dependent on government decisions to survive and prosper, became increasingly vulnerable to political control. In fact, one of the principal reasons for the creation of this system was that it provided the Rhee government with leverage over forces that might otherwise threaten the security and continuity of government.

The Rhee administration was extremely sensitive to political opposition, and its industrial policy was calculated to reduce the independence of the small but growing class of urban entrepreneurs. More threatening to Rhee's political ambitions, however, was the well-established rural elite, the traditional landlord class. This elite espoused a rigid conservatism that had fought every reform from the late nineteenth through the middle of the twentieth century. Whatever his hopes for Korea, Syngman Rhee understood that the landed aristocracy would have to be politically neutralized.

This consideration prompted the Rhee government to launch

a major land redistribution program. Although redistribution was begun before the establishment of the ROK with the U.S. military government's sale of lands owned by the Japanese, it was substantially increased with the Land Reform Act passed in June 1949. This was a major piece of legislation that altered the distribution of capital and land assets in the countryside and politically disarmed the rural conservatives.

Before 1947, only 16.5 percent of all farmers in South Korea were full owners of the land they farmed. After the completion of land reform in 1952, 71.6 percent of all farmers owned the land they tilled. As a consequence, there was a dramatic reduction in outlays for rent and a corresponding escalation in disposable family income. Family income also burgeoned because of increases in production that followed land reform.[8]

Land reform also demonstrated something about the concerns of the U.S. military government. The United States had been involved in land reform efforts in mainland China as early as 1943.[9] After the Nationalist Chinese retreat to Taiwan in 1949, the United States collaborated with the Taipei government to implement a "land to the tiller" program that had its origins in the writings of Sun Yat-sen, the founder of the revolutionary Kuomintang and the man who inspired the 1911 anti-dynastic revolution.

On Taiwan, together with Chinese agronomists and rural reformers, U.S. officials became involved in one of the most rapid, dramatic, and successful land redistribution programs in modern developmental history.[10] When General Douglas MacArthur's military government in Seoul issued a series of ordinances concerning land reform in South Korea, the influence of Taiwan's initiatives was apparent.

U.S. influence in the land reform programs of Asia, and the ROK in particular, was important for several reasons: it demonstrated American concern for equity and agrarian development, and involved a collaborative effort between Americans and Asians to overcome one of the region's most enduring obstacles to economic growth and political democratization. The land reform programs conducted under the auspices of the United States—in Japan, Taiwan, and South Korea—differed from the revolutionary land redistribution of Marxist-Leninist regimes in two ways: there was very little violence, and the rights of property were upheld. Farmers labored on their own land and fully expected to profit thereby.

In the two Koreas, for example, the major difference was that while farm family income increased in the ROK, farm family returns on the collective farms in the DPRK were kept at "rational low levels" to allow the state to accumulate capital and fund the massive investment requirements of industry. In the ROK, because investment capital was not siphoned out of the rural economy, land reform reduced income disparities in the countryside as well as between the rural areas and the urban centers. By 1975 rural household income in the ROK was at least 84 percent of urban per capita income. Because the rural population became an increasingly important component in the modernization process, and the government was responsive to aggregate interests, farmers were provided better access to markets and energy grids by the expansion of road and electrical networks. As a consequence, the standard of life in the countryside steadily improved.

All this served the general process of growth and development. Healthy and educated rural youth could be readily and profitably assimilated into the industrial work force. Moreover, increased rural household incomes provided effective demand for the domestic expansion of light consumer-goods industries.[11] Although land redistribution in South Korea often approximated outright confiscation, the long-term effects were not only more humane than those in the DPRK, they also made major contributions to the nation's economic growth and industrialization. No less important, the United States was instrumental in initiating the land reform program. Thus, despite Marxist rhetoric to the contrary, it was the land reform program conducted under "imperialist" auspices, rather than its communist counterpart, that proved to be humane, progressive, and economically propitious.

*Republic of Korea: Industrialization*

By the end of the 1950s, the government of Syngman Rhee began to lose control of the political situation in the ROK. The

Rhee administration established the First Republic in 1948, defended it against the DPRK invasion between 1950 and 1953, supervised the post-war reconstruction, and promulgated land reform, all with credible results. But too much had been undertaken under authoritarian auspices. Almost all the important national ministries, bureaus, and sections were headed by functionaries appointed by the president. Local government was no less subject to central control, with provincial governors and local leaders being presidential appointees or subject to presidential approval.

The Rhee government insisted that to function efficiently and to maintain national security it had to impose strict control over information and the means of communication, suppress dissidence, and monitor all independent political life in the republic. The net result was a growing sense of political malaise in the ROK and the increasing alienation of its most articulate citizenry.

This alienation created a volatile political environment. Although hard statistics are not available, it appears that, in a relatively stagnant economy, unemployment was particularly high among veterans and university graduates. Moreover, during the election of 1960, charges of irregularities, interference, and corruption were leveled against the Liberal Party of President Rhee. A series of demonstrations expressed the public outrage, and on March 15, the day of the elections, student demonstrations ended in widespread violence. The situation became increasingly incendiary, bloody riots broke out in Seoul, martial law was imposed, and troops were called in to disperse the crowds.

The political unrest troubled all segments of the population, and many feared that the DPRK would embark on a new military adventure to exploit the political instability. President Rhee was urged to make way for a more responsive government, and his administration collapsed.

On July 15, 1960, the incumbent assembly adopted an amendment to the constitution that provided for a cabinet system of government with a bicameral legislature. The newly elected assembly, in joint session, elected Yun Po-sun president of the

Second Republic, and he assumed office on August 15. Chang Myon was selected prime minister, and the Rhee era passed into Korean history.

The life of the Second Republic was brief. The new government had neither the resources nor the initiative to resolve the problems that had accumulated and spread throughout the system. Political unrest continued, and there was evidence that the DPRK was preparing to exploit the situation. On May 16, 1961, Major General Park Chung-hee staged a military coup. By midmorning, a Military Revolution Committee announced that it was assuming the responsibilities of governance.

Between May 1961 and December 1962 the ROK was ruled by martial law. In December 1962, a new constitution, inaugurating the Third Republic, was approved by popular referendum. In the presidential election held in October 1963, General Park, having resigned from the military, was elected president by a popular plurality. In the National Assembly elections that followed, candidates from Park's Democratic Republican Party won a majority of seats, creating a stable environment in which political and economic initiatives could be undertaken with some optimism.

During this period, the ROK's rapid economic growth began. The economic expansion and industrialization were initiated by men whose "supreme aim" was the reunification of the divided peninsula. To do so, it was necessary to "successfully modernize" the ROK, because victory over the enemy, in the last analysis, would be the consequence of successful "economic construction" rather than "military confrontation."[12]

Park Chung-hee believed that political stability was necessary to achieve economic development, and that it was the foremost problem afflicting the Third Republic. The motives behind the drive to modernize and industrialize the ROK—like those of the Koreans at the turn of the century—were exquisitely political.[13] The urgency and emotion that attended the process gave testimony to that. What distinguished the strategies of growth and development in the ROK in the 1960s and 1970s from those of the DPRK or of the reformers of the Yi Dynasty was the conviction that real growth and sustained development could only be accomplished if the nation remained a working, interdependent member of the international economic community.

That conviction carried a number of implications. Not only did it imply accepting foreign aid (North Korea had done as much from other members of the "proletarian community"), but it suggested an involvement in international trade that was excluded by the "anti-imperialist" posturing and the "self-reliant" growth strategies of the Marxist-Leninists of Pyongyang. The trade policy of the Park government implied not only international involvement, but export-led growth through "export promotion."[14] Export promotion, in turn, fostered a number of important collateral developments. With the emphasis on industry, agriculture was somewhat neglected—the government provided little direct investment in the rural economy. But the requirements of export-led growth benefited the farm population almost immediately.

Industrialization for export, for instance, required an elaborate domestic transport and communications infrastructure. The evolving network of roads and rails provided farm-to-market transportation that was cheap and rapid. And because of land reform, farm families had access to the growing income stream.

The results were already evident by the mid-1960s. Between 1955 and 1960, the number of grain processing machines owned by farm families had grown from about 62,000 to about 64,000. Between 1960 and 1985, that number escalated from about 64,000 to about 90,000. The same phenomenon was observed with power pumps, power threshers, and power tillers. In fact, the increases were even more startling. The number of power pumps owned by farm families between 1955 and 1960 had actually decreased—from about 7,500 in 1955 to about 7,000 in 1960. In 1965, five years later, over 26,000 such pumps were in service.[15]

Industrialization in the ROK was not predicated on capital transfers between agrarian and industrializing sectors, as it was in the DPRK. In fact, there was no net cash flow out of the rural areas until the 1970s. Rather than capital, the agrarian sector provided a pool of labor, raw materials, a domestic market, and food products for the developing sector.

The ROK government also made some direct investments in the rural economy. For years the government subsidized necessary farm inputs, such as farm machinery and chemical fertilizers. The government also helped introduce high-yield plant varieties into rural production.

It was only in the early 1970s, however, that a broad program of farm support was initiated. Called the *Saemaul Undong* (New Community Movement), it encouraged rural communities to undertake self-help projects by awarding them small government grants. More important were the price supports for grain that assured farmers predictable returns on their investments. By 1975, as a result, there had been "a dramatic improvement in the quality of life for the rural population. . . . Infant mortality dropped and health conditions improved."[16]

Of course, the decision to pursue an export-led growth strategy had implications beyond the relative neglect of the agrarian sector. To make Korean exports competitive in the world market the inflated national currency had to be devalued, and to fuel the development program, domestic saving and investment had to be encouraged. The artificially low interest rates that seemed appropriate in the economic environment created by the Rhee administration were no longer suitable. As a consequence, between 1961 and 1964, the national currency of the ROK was devalued by almost 50 percent and interest rates on savings were doubled. The proportion of investment financed out of domestic resources in the ROK increased from 30 percent in the biennial 1960–1962 to 100 percent in 1974–1976, reflecting the growth of domestic savings, which expanded from about 3 percent of the GNP in the early 1960s to 27 percent by 1975. Thus, although private consumption in the ROK increased at an average annual rate of 5.3 percent over the fifteen years between 1960 and 1975, South Koreans reduced the percentage of GNP devoted to private consumption from 84.2 percent to 65.7 percent, committing the remainder to domestic capital formation.[17] In general, wages increased at an average annual rate of about 7 percent, and those in manufacturing at an average annual rate of about 8.5 percent.

By the mid-1960s, the Park government had put in place a

comprehensive set of programs to stimulate and sustain exports. Those programs included accelerated depreciation on fixed assets employed by the export industries, tax advantages for export companies, tariff reductions on intermediate capital goods and raw materials used in the production of export items, and discretionary access to credit as well as exchange-rate advantages for major exporting firms. In general, these export-incentive programs were orchestrated and administered by the Korean Trade Promotion Corporation, which was created in 1964 to further international market development. Together with the Economic Planning Board, the Trade Promotion Corporation, and a number of other governmental agencies, the Park administration formulated and implemented a series of Five Year Plans. Although sponsored and supervised by a highly centralized governmental bureaucracy, the plans incorporated inputs from a wide variety of constituencies. The "principal engine" of growth has been, and remains, private enterprise.[18]

Export growth required that ROK commodities successfully compete in the international market. As a result, a premium was placed on quality control and innovation, both of which can best be undertaken by private enterprise responding to market signals. Non-agricultural gross domestic product thus grew at a compound rate of over 13 percent a year from 1961 through 1975, with most of the production decisions being made by the private sector.[19] Those decisions included introducing new goods and new methods of production, pursuing new markets, searching out new sources of supply, and employing new managerial techniques and forms of organization. Spurred by market incentives and government exhortations, ROK entrepreneurs have assiduously sought overseas technology and rewarded inventiveness at home so as to remain at the cutting edge of product marketability.

Out of all this the ROK created a dynamic engine of growth. During the first Five Year Plan (1962–1966), South Korea's total production of goods and services increased at an average annual rate of 7.7 percent. The second Five Year Plan (1967–1971) yielded an average annual rate of 11.3 percent; and the third Five Year Plan (1972–1976) registered an average of 10.9 percent, with 1976 peaking at 15.5 percent. In the fifteen years between 1961 and 1976 the ROK maintained an average annual increase of 9.5 percent and increased the GNP by 400 percent.[20]

One of the most remarkable features of this dynamic growth was that material benefits were more equitably distributed in the ROK than in almost any other developing economy. In World Bank publications and in international forums the ROK is regularly cited as a prime illustration of how all major groups can benefit from rapid growth in national income.[21]

For the workers in the manufacturing industries, wages increased with increments of production. Without union action or legislative enactment, wages rose rapidly, due entirely to market mechanisms; the increasing demand for labor and the ability of labor to relocate to its own advantage led employers to attract workers with wage incentives.

Much the same can be said for the technicians, engineers, and service personnel. The rapid growth of industry fostered steady improvement in the living standards of the general population. Indirectly corroborating this trend is the fact that a substantial part of the ROK's industrial growth was due to escalating domestic demand. At the same time, South Koreans were saving and investing more and more. By 1975, domestic savings represented 21 percent of the ROK's gross national product.

## *The Republic of Korea as a Newly Industrialized Country*

The portion of the ROK labor force employed in agriculture diminished from 63 percent in 1963 to 45 percent in 1976. And by the mid-1970s, manufacturing, construction, and utilities supplied 35 percent, and the service sector 39 percent, of the nation's production of goods and services.[22]

In the interim, changes in the international environment would have a major impact on the political leadership in Seoul. Park Chung-hee had made it eminently clear that the economic development of the nation was necessary to win ultimate sovereignty and achieve reunification. He was equally convinced that the resulting Korea would have to be non-communist if economic well-being and political liberty were to exist.[23] Park thus committed a ROK combat force to help defend the Republic of

Vietnam during the Vietnam War. The Republic of Korea conceived of itself as a member of an anti-communist security confederation dedicated to containing and ultimately defeating Marxism-Leninism in East and Southeast Asia.

Developments after 1969 generated considerable tension among members of that real or fancied confederation. In 1969, with the United States weary of its involvement in Vietnam, President Richard Nixon, in the so-called "Guam Doctrine," announced that he would no longer provide ground troops for the defense of Asian nations. The United States would maintain forward-deployed air and naval units, but the immediate security of the non-communist nations would be their own responsibility.

Many Asians understood this as part of a U.S. effort to disengage. There were disturbing signals that Americans felt overextended by their security commitments to their Asian allies. The Vietnam conflict had generated political dissension within the United States, leaving Washington little disposed to become involved in any further conflict in Asia.

At almost the same time, the Nixon administration made overtures to the communist regime in Beijing for a normalization of diplomatic relations—at the expense of the Republic of China on Taiwan, one of Washington's security partners in the region. Taken together, these developments seriously undermined the credibility of the U.S. security guarantee for the Republic of Korea. The ROK leadership thus decided that the nation must more adequately provide for its own security. That would involve two major undertakings: (1) tightening political controls to ensure domestic stability, and (2) accelerating the pace of industrialization, including expansion of heavy industries critical to self-defense.[24]

As a result, a new constitution, the so-called *Yushin* (or Revitalizing) Constitution, was promulgated in 1972. It marked the birth of the Fourth Republic and reinforced the authoritarian and hierarchical features of the ROK polity.

As part of the program of increased self-reliance, gross capital investment was redirected into heavy industry. By the mid-1970s capital investment in heavy industry was increasing at an annual rate of 26 percent per annum, a significant change in developmental policy.[25]

By the time President Jimmy Carter announced his decision to withdraw U.S. ground forces from South Korea in 1977, the Park administration had thoroughly committed itself to a major economic program designed to create an industrial base sufficiently strong to provide for the country's own defense.

The new program required a very rapid increase in the availability of capital funds. Much of it was provided by government printing presses, and the funds were made available at negative real interest rates. More capital was borrowed in the international financial markets. The result was domestic inflation and a rapid increase in the nation's external debt. The foreign debt, less than $2 billion in 1970, escalated to about $20 billion by the end of the decade.

During this time oil prices were rising dramatically, compounding the import burdens on the economy. The second round of price increases at the end of the decade proved particularly damaging, and in 1980, for the first time since 1961, the economy of the ROK collapsed into negative growth—the gross national output decreased by 5.2 percent from the preceding year, and the trade account hit a record deficit of $4.6 billion.

The entire economy had been caught up in a spiral of inflationary pressure, and both security and well-being were threatened. Political resistance to Park's authoritarianism began to mount, reinforced by the system dysfunction. On the night of October 26, 1979, Park Chung-hee was assassinated and Prime Minister Choi Kyu-hah assumed the presidency. Once again, the military moved to control the deteriorating political and economic situation. In August 1980, General Chun Doo-hwan, commanding general of the Defense Security Forces, resigned his military commission and was elected president by the National Conference for Unification. In October, a new constitution was promulgated, marking the establishment of the Fifth Republic.

President Chun imposed austerity measures that reduced inflation to manageable levels, and the economy of the republic recommenced its self-sustained growth. In 1982, the economy achieved a 5.6 percent rate of real growth, followed by a 9.0

percent rate in 1983, 7.6 percent in 1984, 5.1 percent in 1985, and over 8.0 percent in 1986. Export expansion resumed at a rate of over 25 percent per annum by the mid-1980s. By that time, the heavy industries established at such great cost during the 1970s matured into production. By 1985, for example, Hyundai Motor Company emerged as the principal supplier of passenger cars to Canada, surpassing Toyota and Honda. Exports of ROK automobiles to the United States that same year exceeded 100,000 sales. Achievements in the export of semiconductors have been equally impressive. Although lagging behind the principal producers in Japan and the United States, ROK firms have been closing the technological gap. ROK industry has become the leading manufacturer of large-scale integrated circuits, and two ROK firms—Hyundai Electronics and Samsung Semiconductor and Telecommunications—are producing world-class electronic chips. By 1982 the electronics industry accounted for 6 percent of the nation's GNP and 10 percent of its exports.

To sustain its present success, authorities have underwritten a rapid expansion of domestic research and development facilities and increased outlays for upgrading scientific and technological capabilities. In 1973, the government created a National Council for Science and Technology and in 1981 it funded a venture capital company, the Korean Technology Development Corporation, establishing a link between technology development and its use in industrial production.

In all this, the authorities in Seoul have responded to clear imperatives. As per capita income has increased, the comparative advantage of the low wage costs long enjoyed by ROK manufacturers has been correspondingly reduced. Higher labor costs have thus added to the export price of commodities and spurred the use of labor-saving automated processes. Automation has in turn generated an increased need for trained manpower in research, development, and maintenance. The ROK has embarked upon a course that will lead to advanced industrialization.

As the ROK economy stabilized after the early 1980s recession, unemployment declined to frictional levels, gravitating to a level of 3.5 percent of the labor force. Given that situation, and the price supports supplied to the agricultural sector, domestic demand has provided much of the incentive for renewed economic expansion.

These factors have all contributed to the overall improvement in the quality of life in the ROK. Educational opportunities have increased along with wage rates, allowing more students to pursue advanced studies. More and more products have become available, and more public aid is being directed to social development. The ROK government has embarked on social programs to relieve prevailing housing shortages, improve the delivery of health care, enlarge existing health insurance programs, and improve the national welfare and pension programs.

The pattern is intrinsically good. As the economy of the ROK has grown in size and complexity, the government has allowed market forces a greater role in allocating resources and setting the course of economic development. Over the past quarter century, the ROK economy has deepened and matured. ROK industry has shown a readiness and a capacity to respond to changes in industrial technology. Innovations in design and engineering, especially those using microprocessors, have allowed manufacturers of skill-intensive products to enter markets hitherto closed to relatively small and less-developed countries.

All major population segments have benefited from this expansion. The ROK is an exemplary instance of how growth can be achieved with equity. Although industrial concentration and income disparities between skilled and unskilled labor may have increased material inequalities in the immediate past, relative income equity is generally a singular feature of the ROK developmental experience.

*U.S. Interests and Policy*

The extraordinary economic performance of the Republic of Korea provides evidence that the judgment of the United States concerning economic development in the less-developed regions of the globe is fundamentally correct. Most Americans hold that economic development can best be achieved when market mechanisms are permitted to function. Americans are equally convinced that command economies characteristically malfunction and are cost inefficient and egregiously wasteful.

In the more than four decades since the end of World War II, the superiority of market-governed systems has been demonstrated any number of times. The economy of West Germany is superior to that of East Germany, that of Taiwan superior to that of the PRC, and so on. But in no instance has the superiority of market-governed systems been clearer than in Korea. The ROK economy is among the most advanced in Asia, with a per capita income superior to that of any country in the region under Marxist-Leninist governance. The ROK has accomplished everything for which its reformers and revolutionaries struggled at the turn of the century. It is well on the way to becoming a major industrial power.

Moreover, the ROK embarked on its growth program with the assistance and collaboration of the United States. Not only did the United States provide security for the ROK, it provided a massive transfer of goods and capital before and during the Korean conflict. The economic aid lavished for ten years after the war rescued a traumatized population from destitution and supplied the material foundation for its economic development. The $2.6 billion in direct aid provided between 1953 and 1961, and the $2.6 billion supplied from 1962 through 1976, left the ROK economy solvent.

Furthermore, the entire process of development took place within the framework of the international trading and financial community, shattering one of the articles of faith of Marxist-Leninist and "progressive" academics. For decades they have held that less-developed communities are forever condemned to underdevelopment if growth is attempted within the confines of the "international capitalist community."

In fact, the ROK has been successful in every way that the DPRK has failed. Animated by a vision akin to that of most Americans, the ROK people have developed and industrialized their economy, in the course of which the benefits have been abundantly available and equitably distributed.

During the process, U.S. consumers have enjoyed inexpensive and attractive Korean products while U.S. farmers and manufacturers have exported substantial quantities of agricultural and high technology goods to ROK consumers. Whatever the tensions generated by U.S. and South Korean trade disagreements, they must be considered within the context of a long and mutually beneficial relationship. This success story has not been lost on developing countries in Asia, Latin America, and Africa. The 1980s have seen a dramatic shift among these countries away from developmental strategies that involve central planning. More and more countries are pursuing policies that allow market signals to govern economic growth and development, undeniably a major contribution to U.S. foreign policy interests.

Finally, the United States has long defended market-based economies not only because of their fundamental efficiency and productiveness, but because Americans believe that free markets foster individual freedom and help create the political culture of liberal democracy. In the American view, a bureaucratically controlled economy supplies the bone and sinew of totalitarian systems, while market-based economies nurture political pluralism. The final measure of U.S. concern for the ROK turns on that country's promise of political democracy—a by-product of its astonishing economic development.

# 3

# *Political Development*

THE TWENTIETH CENTURY has witnessed rapid increases in population, escalating conflicts, social revolution, and major economic change. The resulting dislocations have taxed the ability of political systems to respond successfully. Established modes of behavior were inadequate, causing traditional autocracies, monarchies, and sheikdoms to collapse. Dynasties that originated before the advent of the common era were overthrown to make way for more modern forms of government.

As a concept, "political modernization" is as familiar as it is vague and complex, and it is frequently used interchangeably with "political development." For our purposes, "political development" will be used to refer to the increasing capacity of a political system to meet the challenges of the modern period—to manage growing populations in environments of rapid economic development, extensive technological change, and accelerated industrialization.

Modern political systems need to manifest greater *differentiation* than more traditional systems. Changing environmental demands necessitate new government agencies and increasing diversity among those that already exist. Where traditional governments were concerned largely with the defense of life and property and the collection of taxes, modern systems have been charged with a variety of complex obligations, including economic management, population control, general education, and policy formulation.

How successfully modern political systems discharge those

obligations is a measure of their efficacy. The most ineffective fail to satisfy minimum system maintenance requirements and collapse under cross pressures. Some remain politically unstable but survive nonetheless. Some fail to initiate, sustain, and manage economic growth and succumb to foreign aggression or internal disintegration. Others achieve a sufficient level of growth to maintain the basic integrity of the political system but little else.

Finally, because the modern period has been characterized by any number of new cognitive and skill requirements, previous class and caste restrictions against employing certain individuals and groups have proved dysfunctional. Developing economic systems make special demands on populations and need to search out talent wherever it might be found. Talent replaces heritage and status as the requirement for upward social mobility, differential employment, and access to system benefits and responsibilities.

All of this translates into the demand for equality of opportunity and treatment. The demand for *equality* becomes the political expression of system needs.

When Western Europe underwent the trauma of the Industrial Revolution, the demand for equality accompanied the rise of the new entrepreneurial and industrial classes. The urban representatives who supplied the necessary talent for the new economic systems voiced several non-traditional political demands. Intellectuals provided the rationale for the new demands, and the rising class of propertied entrepreneurs supplied much of the material support for the new systems.

In sum, political development can best be discussed by employing the three major concepts of differentiation, efficacy, and equality.[1] Modern political systems are effective if they are sufficiently differentiated to satisfy the dynamic demands of economic growth and industrialization. Differentiation and efficacy require the equality of opportunity and access that allows talent to satisfy the new demands created by the complex changes taking place.

How successfully any system meets these challenges that

characterize the modern period is a measure of its degree of "modernization."

*Marxism and Development*

Marxism bears a curious relationship to development. On the one hand, the founders of Marxism, Karl Marx and Friedrich Engels, conceived of their system as satisfying the requirements of the modern epoch. On the other hand, they had little idea of what those requirements would actually be.

While Marx and Engels believed that their revolutionary notions responded to problems generated by economic development and industrialization, they understood them to be postindustrial issues, one of the most important being the inability of the capitalist system to distribute its abundance profitably. For both Marx and Engels, world capitalism had run its course by the last half of the nineteenth century. As early as the *Communist Manifesto* (1848), they wrote that capitalism had become a "fetter" on any further economic or social development.

Marx and Engels argued that the conglomerate industries of mature capitalism had produced so great an abundance of urban factory workers that they made up the "vast majority" of the population of the Western world. Capitalism's massive industries, which could produce commodities in enormous abundance, required enormous sums for their start-up and maintenance. But because those enterprises were so capital intensive, they could provide only subsistence wages to their workers. As a result, the system could not provide sufficient demand to clear capitalist inventories at a profit. Periodically, the system would enter into a crisis of overproduction (or underconsumption) and all productive activity would cease. Workers would be driven into the "reserve army of labor."

These episodic crises would get deeper and deeper, and more and more workers would be faced with the alternative of revolution or starvation. Ultimately, the "vast majority" would rise up and dispossess their oppressors. Production would be undertaken for use and not for profit. Unconstrained by the need to produce capitalist profit, the industrial system would generate unlimited abundance.

In the course of this process, the rising "bourgeoisie" had allowed talent to make its necessary contributions, but as the system matured, inequalities began to accumulate. By their own time, Marx and Engels insisted, capitalism had institutionalized inequities to such an extent that it was denying itself the talents locked up in the working classes.

The system survived only because of decreasing competition. Inefficiencies and waste increased. Fewer and fewer capitalists owned more and more of the productive system in a vast interconnected web of monopolies, and they maintained profit levels by their control over supply. The efficacy of the system was seriously compromised.

At the same time, the working classes were being inadequately trained to the tasks of the industrial system. Private ownership and the stratified nature of the mature system obstructed the realization of their productive potential.

Through the socialist revolution, the working class would seize the means of production. Without private ownership and the desire for profit, the working class could distribute the abundance of industrial production to each "according to his need," and the full talents of the working classes could be applied to production—"from each according to his abilities."

The political state would then proceed to "wither away." There would no longer be any need for the exercise of political governance. Only the mangement of production would be necessary and that would be undertaken by the workers. Political leadership would be provided by the rotation in office of simple workmen. The system would be differentiated, effective, and egalitarian.[2] This was the vision that inspired V. I. Lenin and the first Bolsheviks.

*Stalinism and Development*

Unhappily, once classical Marxism was transformed into a strategy for rapid economic development and industrialization, everything changed. The Marxism of Stalin was fundamentally different from that of Marx and Engels. In a post-revolutionary society composed largely of agrarians—who had no industrial skills and were forced to do work assigned to them by some central planning agency—all the concepts advanced by Marx and Engels had to be abandoned.

For those who attempt to develop economically retarded communities, scarce skills and capital become critically important. Government, under the goad of development and faced by a shortfall in available talent and capital, becomes increasingly responsible for the performance of complex allocative tasks. A developmental strategy involving central planning in an essentially non-industrial environment imposes further burdens. A huge bureaucracy results, exercising increasingly arbitrary and intrusive control over vast populations. Equality is sacrificed to differentiation and efficacy. Central planners assume allocative responsibilities, bureaucrats become their privileged agents, and the general population becomes subject to draconian control.

Thus the Soviet Union under Stalin, and the DPRK under Kim Il-sung. Not only do such systems radically depart from the normative expectations of classical Marxism, they justify themselves with a peculiar rationale.

Marx and Engels conceived their post-revolutionary society as manifestly democratic, with the vast majority equipped to rule. The workers in each industry were deemed capable of handling production. Given production for use, the several industries would merge into one universal enterprise, and production according to "one central plan" would ensue.

When revolutionaries came face to face with tasks for which classical Marxism had not prepared them, however, they were obliged to improvise. Because of the dearth of capital, Marxist leaders took complete control over wages, availability of consumer goods, and the allocation of resources, and they determined the pace of growth in the agrarian, industrial, and service sectors of their respective economies. The Marxist-Leninist systems of our time became increasingly hierarchical, and the tenure of their leaders has been so protracted that most of them have died in office.

To sustain the massive effort, and to provide some non-material compensation for exacting labor, these systems have created an environment charged with emotion. The revolution is freighted with the responsibilities of "history" and captained by a unique "leader" of "genius," and masses are inspired to sacrificial effort by "slogans" in vast "campaigns."

Stalin was the leader who forced the masses of backward Russia along the path of economic growth and industrial development. He abandoned equality in the pursuit of differentiation and system efficacy. People of talent assumed onerous responsibilities and enjoyed corresponding benefits. The working class was enjoined to work, to sacrifice, and to obey.

Below the leader and his party, an immense bureaucracy flourished. In a system without recourse to market signals, decisions must somehow be calculated. Prices and wages must be assigned, production quotas determined, and fulfillment monitored. Resource allocation, saving rates, and other priorities must be established. Only those of special genius, possessed of the knowledge of some special "science," could accomplish this. The leader and the vanguard party become linchpins of the system. Thus Fidel Castro became the "Maximum Leader" of the Cuban revolution, Mao Zedong the "Never Setting Red Sun" of the Chinese revolution, and Kim Il-sung the "Leader of Extraordinary Greatness" for the DPRK. "In the very earliest days of revolutionary activity," according to his official biographer, "he gathered around him steadfast fighters, and educated and trained them in his own revolutionary style [in order] to found a Marxist-Leninist party for accomplishing socialism and communism in Korea." Thereafter he continued "to temper the party organizationally and ideologically." With this instrument, Kim Il-sung proceeded to "scientifically identify every question" that was "ripe for solution." The result allows "Comrade Kim Il-sung to be invincible and perform . . . superhuman miracles everywhere. . . ."[3] The epochal transformation of society and of nature itself achieved in the North are wholly attributed to the brilliant leadership of Kim Il-sung and to the vanguard role of the Workers' Party of Korea.

*North Korea and Neo-Stalinism*

The rationale used to legitimate the hegemonic rule of Kim Il-sung and the Korean Workers' Party appeals to "the most scientific theory showing the way to complete class liberation" and to "the construction of a boundlessly prospering ideal society of mankind." The "most scientific theory" is Marxism-Leninism ("only Marxism-Leninism could chart a correct course"), and Kim Il-sung is recognized as "the most outstanding Marxist-Leninist with whom no other leader of any country can compare."[4]

As for the party, it is "armed with the ideas of the political leader who is equipped with the highest knowledge of the law-governed nature of historical development." The constitution of the DPRK maintains that the integrity of the state "relies on the politico-ideological unity of the entire people," which is predicated on the "creative application of Marxism-Leninism."[5]

What results is the creation of a citizenry animated by "devoted fidelity to their leader, party, state, and system." Whatever nominal rights are accorded those people, the DPRK constitution obliges all citizens to observe "the socialist norm of life and the socialist rules of conduct." Citizens are also required to "heighten their revolutionary vigilance against all maneuvers of" those "hostile elements who are opposed to [the] socialist system," a system identified without equivocation as "the dictatorship of the proletariat."[6]

By the time of the Third Party Congress of the Korean Workers' Party in April 1956, Kim Il-sung had put together the fundamental institutions of a Marxist-Leninist state, and by purging all his real or imagined enemies had arrogated to himself all major decision-making powers. In turn, the party, a "unified central structure armed with a consciousness as solid as marble" and "strict rules," controlled the subordinate "political organizations such as state organs, workers' associations, and social associations" in order to marshal the "masses" behind the party.[7]

Of all the Marxist-Leninist states, the DPRK is one of the most totalitarian. The commitment to "democratic centralism," by which all subordinate bodies submit to the decisions rendered by the Standing Committee of the party's Central Committee, ensures a unity and homogeneity deemed essential to a "socialist society."[8]

Thus, while a catalog of formal political rights are incorporated in the constitution, none of them can be exercised. Although the constitution speaks of citizens enjoying the "right to elect and be elected . . . irrespective of sex, race, occupation, length of residence, property status and education, party affiliation, political views, and religion" (Article 52), survey data indicate that the Supreme People's Assembly, the putative legislative organ of the state, is composed almost exclusively of members of the Korean Workers' Party. Moreover, according to law, only a single candidate can run in the single member districts. In theory, the single candidates are elected by assemblies in local enterprises, social organizations, and villages. In fact, the delegates are selected by the Korean Workers' Party.[9]

Article 53 of the constitution further accords citizens "the freedoms of speech, the press, assembly, association, and demonstration." In fact, the communist state celebrates the fact that "a unitary ideological system" prevails in North Korea. Kim Il-sung has insisted that fostering "the ideological revolution" is the most important responsibility of the Korean Workers' Party. Under its ministrations, "the survivals of outdated ideas" in the "minds of the working people" are systematically expunged. The masses require "remolding," without which the "complete victory of socialism" would be impossible.[10]

Thus education must be in the hands of "good communists and revolutionaries," just as the printed word must be employed to further the "revolution" and the people must be protected from "rotten bourgeois" materials. All cultural products, moreover, must contain a "high level of ideological content." Literature and art are part of the "search for truth," a truth found only in "communism and communist society."[11]

To this end, all aspects of literature and art, all print and broadcast media, indeed all sources of information are under strict control. Foreign publications are entirely excluded, and those individuals caught listening to foreign broadcasts are severely punished.

The other social, civil, and political rights "guaranteed" by the constitution are equally spurious. Promises of freedom of association notwithstanding, DPRK citizens are required during their leisure time to participate in organized collective activities. As early as nursery school, children are immersed in indoctrination programs. After school hours, students must participate in political study and self-criticism sessions to improve their revolutionary consciousness and socialist commitment. Compulsory membership in workers' associations and social and civil groups completes the picture.

As part of the regimentation, almost all movement is under surveillance. All travel requires police documents and government permission, and emigration is, of course, illegal.

Every person in the DPRK, moreover, is registered as a member of one of fifty-one categories based on the family's "class background." An individual's category affects access to welfare, schooling, travel, and social mobility. The DPRK social system, although presumably predicated on equality, has in fact become stratified by invidious hereditary political distinctions. Although it is impossible to obtain hard data, hundreds of thousands, perhaps millions, of DPRK citizens of suspect background have undergone "thought reform" and "redemption" through labor camps.

The authorities in Pyongyang have systematically refused to allow any inquiry into political imprisonment and human rights violations in the DPRK. It is nonetheless known that the Ministry of Public Security administers special statutes, whose particulars are secret, to combat "state crimes." Anyone considered untrustworthy by the authorities becomes subject to detainment and prosecution,[12] for the state is required to "defend the socialist system against the subversive activities of hostile elements at home and abroad" (Article 11).

Like all systems in which exclusive political rule is legitimized by a privileged access to some impeccable, universal "Truth," the DPRK exercises totalitarian control over the lives of its citizens. That Truth must be insulated from all criticism, and its defense is therefore perceived not only as a moral imperative but also as a practical one. The very nature of the system requires absolute control over a subject population. Its ideology constitutes its license to rule.

The political development of the DPRK has conformed to the

model first contrived by Stalin in the 1930s. Of all neo-Stalinist systems, it is perhaps most faithful to the original. The DPRK's response to the need for differentiation was to create agencies by fiat, and for the first years of the regime these agencies apparently functioned with some efficiency. The requirements of economic growth and industrial development were met and real expansion was sustained until the mid-1960s. Difficulties began to emerge as the economy grew in complexity. As economies mature, direction and control become increasingly difficult. In the United States in the mid-1960s, for example, the railroad industry required no fewer than 43 *trillion* separate pricing decisions in order to remain reasonably efficient, competitive, and profitable.[13] Given the present geometric increase in system complexity, command economies have shown an inability to govern themselves effectively and efficiently. All have been driven to attempt reform and "restructuring." The DPRK has also attempted reform, but with little success.

What the regime in North Korea has accomplished is stability. The DPRK is one of the most stable regimes in Asia. Kim Il-sung has ruled without significant opposition for some forty years—one of the longest-lived dictators of the century.

In the process, equality has been sacrificed. Not only has the rule of the party precluded political equality, but the inefficiencies of the regime have made for sharp income inequality. More important, political constraints on mobility and recruitment limit the ability of the talented to contribute to the system.

The DPRK system, moreover, has failed to respond effectively to collective needs. While the command economy was able to respond to productive needs during the first decade of development, by the end of the 1960s, the increasing complexities were overwhelming its capacity to react.[14]

In non-market systems, the escalating inefficiency produces fitful attempts at reforms, but the more comprehensive the reforms, the more they threaten the stability of the system—and the hegemonic party. As a result, whatever reforms are undertaken tend to be marginal and non-systemic.

In Asia, these developments have manifested themselves in dramatic fashion. Communist China, communist North Korea, and communist Vietnam display all the species traits and are afflicted with all the system disabilities common to Marxist-Leninist polities. These communist countries are disadvantaged in all the ways that non-communist Taiwan and South Korea are not. The differences that distinguish market and non-market systems are revealed not only in those features we have considered, but in economic growth, income distribution, and factor productivity statistics.

The differences in political development that characterize the DPRK and the ROK are derived from the ideological convictions that animate each, and they originated in the early twentieth century when Koreans were facing the challenges of the new epoch. As early as the eighteenth century, Western learning *(Sohak)* had begun to influence some of Korea's most aggressive intellectuals. Scholars like Yi Ik and An Chong-bok were consumed by an interest in the "practical wisdom" of the West, particularly Western science and technology. By the end of the century, Korean reformers were advocating the rational administration of public affairs at the expense of the "irrationalities" of traditional feudal institutions. Discussion increasingly turned on how political and social organizations could be more effectively used in agriculture, commerce, and industry.[15] What emerged from the ferment was "modernism" within the confines of the decaying Yi Dynasty—and the seeds of a new and democratic Korea.

*Democratic Thought in South Korea*

Both governments on the Korean peninsula received their inspiration from the West. The totalitarianism of the DPRK stems from the nineteenth-century ideas of Marx and Engels via Stalin, while the leaders of the ROK espouse a political system that traces its roots to the liberal democracy of nineteenth-century Europe and North America.

As the Yi Dynasty began to disintegrate in the nineteenth century under internal and external pressures, an aggressive minority of Koreans sought to defend against what they saw as a threat to the very survival of the historical and cultural Korea.

They believed that through "self-strengthening," Korea could resist foreign predators and ensure national continuity.

In this they shared the concerns and much the same strategies as reformers throughout Asia, such as the Meiji reformers of Japan, the reformers of Qing China, and even those of the Philippine archipelago. As a consequence, there was constant cross-fertilization of ideas. If Asia was to survive as an independent center of civilization made up of sovereign states, Asians would have to redress the inadequacies that rendered the entire region vulnerable.

Asian governments were deficient in any number of ways. Inefficient bureaucracies governed passive populations more loyal to a particular locale than to a national community. Effete monarchies persisted in traditional behaviors, defenses, and economies. But no longer able to mobilize enthusiasm or talent, the dynasties of China and Korea gradually lapsed into fatal lethargy.

Asian reformers were fascinated by the vitality, productivity, and military capabilities of the West. They identified Western drive with a popular involvement in governing the community. In dynastic China, both Liang Ch'i-ch'ao (Liang Qichao) and Sun Yat-sen advocated major reforms to render the government more responsive to the people. They began to back political "populism" well before the end of the nineteenth century. By the beginning of the twentieth century, they were arguing for the extension of civil and political rights to all Chinese citizens so as to stimulate the economic growth and industrialization of the nation, which they saw as the necessary conditions for China's survival in the face of Western imperialism. Political democracy and industrial capitalism would save their threatened national community.

Since citizen involvement presupposed citizen training and popular education, Liang argued that Chinese publications, available only in stylized traditional form, be rendered in the vernacular. This would interest citizens in public affairs, make education more available, and upgrade the skills of the general population, thus strengthening the entire nation. Sun Yat-sen repeated much of the argument of men like Liang, and added advocacy of a program of rapid agricultural and industrial growth and development.[16] These same themes appear in the writings of any number of Asian reformers of the period. In effect, political democracy and market-governed economic development made up the first coherent Asian response to the crises of the late nineteenth and early twentieth century.

Among Koreans, it was essentially the same. Korean concern with the practical application of learning (the *Silhak* movement) began as early as the late seventeenth century. It matured into a nineteenth century movement that advocated the rationalization of administrative practice, the development of material science, and the accelerated growth of the economy.[17]

Of particular importance was the work of the remarkable So Che-pil (known to Americans as Philip Jaisohn).[18] Educated in the United States between 1885 and 1895, So returned to Korea to undertake a program of education and political agitation intended to raise the social and political consciousness of his people.

Like Liang Ch'i-ch'ao, So was convinced that public participation in community affairs was absolutely essential to sovereignty and survival. He became an apostle for civil and political rights, mass education, and economic development. He became the editor of the successful and influential publication *The Independent* and founder of the Independence Club, a reformist, activist, and educational organization committed to rehabilitating a decadent Korea through democratic practice and institutions.[19]

These ideas made up the intellectual substance of the noncommunist Korean nationalist movement throughout the period of Japanese occupation of the peninsula and animated the noncommunist leadership that came to power in South Korea with the defeat of Japan in 1945. Whatever his disabilities, Syngman Rhee brought with him the legacy of democratic and nationalist commitments we find among the reformers and revolutionaries of the turn of the century.[20]

*Political Development in South Korea*

The Korean situation in 1945 was enormously complicated, not only because of the presence of mutually suspicious bodies of foreign troops, but because the Korean political activists who returned with the American troops were both democratic and nationalist. They believed in democracy, at least in part, because they saw it as a source of strength for the non-communist cause.

Political democracy, with all its implied institutional and procedural features, was considered instrumental to the security, survival, and international status of their nation. Nonetheless, it had always been evident that the leaders of the democratic nationalist movement would not sacrifice the security of their nation for the sake of an ideal democracy. All this Syngman Rhee had made clear from the moment he returned to Korea after the liberation in 1945.

The political creed that constituted the rationale for his life's activities was nonetheless fundamentally democratic in character. Rhee, and the others who acceded to power in the ROK, created widespread democratic expectations among Koreans that, in effect, became promissory notes on the future. Satisfaction of those expectations might be delayed, but as the recent history of the ROK indicates, they are not to be denied.

The first ROK constitution, promulgated in 1948, was essentially democratic in character, although it had more features in common with Continental than with American practice. Its catalog of political and civil liberties is typical of democratic practice. The potential restrictions on those liberties were no more portentous, in principle, than those in the French or Italian constitutions.

The increasingly authoritarian character of the ROK government was largely due to Rhee's legitimate fear of attack from the North, as well as concern for his own political future. But the differences between the authoritarianism of the South and the totalitarianism of the North were evident from the start.

In the May 1950 elections in the ROK, for example, many of Rhee's opponents won seats. In fact, the existence of an active opposition contributed to Kim Il-sung's decision to invade the South. No such political opposition could survive in the DPRK.

After the war, Rhee continued to feel insecure, and for good reason. Rhee, like many other leaders in our time, was convinced that he was indispensable to the security of the republic and attempted to ensure his continued rule by revising the constitution. At the same time, the democratic expectations of Koreans quickened, in part through Rhee's own appeals to democractic norms. Thus, even after the Korean conflict had revealed the vulnerabilities of the ROK, a broad-based opposition to Rhee continued. In 1956, the opposition Democratic Party candidate, Chang Myon, was elected vice president of the republic. So powerful was that opposition that when Rhee's followers attempted to manipulate the ballot counting in the March 1960 elections, student demonstrations compelled the weakened Rhee to step down.

Thus, even under the authoritarianism of Rhee, a formal political opposition not only survived but prevailed in South Korea. No one could possibly suggest that an organized political opposition could have existed in post-1950 North Korea.

The distinction is best captured by recognizing that the ROK government is legitimized, in the final analysis, by a democratic rationale. Departures from political democracy are justified as temporary responses to emergency conditions. The DPRK government, on the other hand, is totalitarian and its derogations of democratic values are not departures from, but embodiments of, its convictions. The rulers of the DPRK legitimize their right to rule by insisting that they possess a truth truer than true: Marxism-Leninism as creed.

The ROK can arguably be conceived as a political democracy operating under emergency constraints. The DPRK, on the other hand, is an *ideocracy*—a regime whose rule is legitimized by virtue of a gifted leadership capable of applying the insights of an obscure social theory to the Korean peninsula.[21]

For the quarter century following the collapse of the Rhee administration, the ROK government displayed the same ambivalence that attended the birth of the republic. The military coup of Major General Park Chung-hee in 1961 was followed by a series of authoritarian measures that stabilized the South and began its trajectory of rapid growth. Park Chung-hee, in fact, was so closely associated with the phenomenal economic growth and modernization of the ROK that he has been called "the architect of the economic miracle."[22]

Between 1961 and 1970, the Park government articulated a complex administrative structure that stabilized the political situation and inaugurated a new economic policy. Employing emergency powers, he banned thousands of politicians from political activity and imposed controls on information. A new political party, the Democratic Republic Party, was launched to provide a civilian vehicle for the new military leadership. More significantly, the government decided that an economic strategy predicated on import substitution had exhausted its possibilities and that therefore exports must be expanded. The new economic policy emphasized the role of market mechanisms in organizing growth activity.

Like the Republic of China on Taiwan, the ROK undertook a program of rapid growth and industrialization employing the market as an instrument of developmental planning, a "revolution in practical economic thought." This was in contrast to the then-current belief that economic policy in less-developed countries should be based on centralized planning, or "taut planning."[23]

Between 1961 and his death in 1979, Park Chung-hee supervised the construction of an elaborate system of agencies devoted to macro and sectoral economic planning. By the end of the 1960s, there were complex interrelations between many governmental and non-governmental bodies. The Economic Planning Board (EPB), which had formal responsibility for national planning, provided the Five Year Plan's basic outline. The Ministry of State Enterprises—responsible for about 30 percent of the nation's fixed capital formation in the fertilizer, iron, steel, and power industries as well as in railroads and financial institutions—developed its own, compatible, planning proposals. The ministries of Commerce and Industry, of Finance, of Agriculture and Fisheries, and of Transportation and Communications submitted their own proposals as well.

Around these ministries, a number of advisory committees collected. Initially, there were twenty-five attached to the Ministry of Commerce and Industry, twenty to Finance, twelve to Agriculture, and twenty-nine to Transportation and Communications. These advisory committees, originally suggested by

American advocates of participatory public service, became increasingly important in the planning process. They brought aggressive and talented leaders of the economic community into close collaboration with the government. These individuals were chosen almost exclusively because of their achievements. Political considerations had little influence on selection.

By the mid-1970s, this complex planning structure had been consolidated. Not only had the advisory committees become smaller and more efficient, their bureaucratic counterparts were increasingly staffed by younger, more capable, and better educated members from rural, poor, and working-class backgrounds.[24]

However authoritarian and centralized the system, it had created a growth program that was among the most efficient in the developing world. The system was efficient in large part because market mechanisms signaled gross inefficiencies as well as sectoral and investment imbalance. Thus, current, relevant, and correct data were available to planners. Individual government policies could be changed as circumstances changed. By the early 1980s, as a case in point, government-sponsored laws and regulations were being generated at the rate of one thousand a year. Within the space of a year, however, more than 10 percent of those laws and regulations were revised at least twice. Today, the ROK government carefully monitors economic indices and undertakes an annual economic management review and evaluation of performance. It is distinguished among developing countries by the flexibility and responsiveness of its planning.[25]

Throughout these developments, the specifically political system remained authoritarian, although never so repressive that a political opposition could not survive. Even Park Chung-hee, in the elections of 1963, 1967, and 1971, could prevail only with narrow victories. He was forced to control the National Assembly with a minority of total votes. Moreover, in the post-Park period, three major opposition parties opposed the Chun Doohwan administration, and with considerable success. In the March 1981 general elections, the government party won only 35 percent of the popular vote, and in the February 1985 elections, the three opposition parties received 58 percent of the popular vote to the ruling party's 35 percent. Unlike in the North, the ultimate legitimation for political rule in the South is through contested elections. The employment of emergency powers always remains precisely that—a temporary reaction to a crisis.

The economic development of the ROK is outward oriented and market governed by design. The ROK is eminently penetrable. Koreans must travel to obtain training and skills, explore foreign demand preferences, secure international market shares, and attract foreign investments. Foreigners must visit the ROK to place orders, inspect inventories, establish business contacts, provide managerial instruction, and service transferred technologies.

As a consequence, the ROK is sensitive to international public opinion; it cannot exclude foreign publications, foreign values, and foreign ideas, all of which have penetrated the intellectual environment of the nation.

The two Koreas have developed politically in distinctive fashions. The DPRK has created a system with enough differentiation and efficiency to assure material adequacy to its population, and an institutional stability unmatched almost anywhere in Asia. But in the process, further differentiation and efficacy have been impaired, and equality and opportunity have been sacrificed. "Class" identification has created invidious distinctions, denying individuals equality before the law as well as many civil and political rights. The rights of voluntary association, expression, conviction, choice, and personal security are nonexistent.

The ROK, for its part, has built a system of remarkable efficiency and differentiation. It has sustained a rate of economic growth and a distribution of income superior to that of almost any other developing nation. There is also considerable upward mobility and relative equality of opportunity. The derogation of civil and political rights has been serious, but it is incomparably less systematic, extensive, and protracted than that in the DPRK.

The flaws of the ROK in terms of political development are correctable, in principle, within the system. For example, the large industrial conglomerates, the so-called *chaebol,* which are responsible for about 31 percent of the value added in the manufacturing sector and 17 percent of the value added in total ROK output, have received government favor at the expense of the smaller enterprises. Most of the leadership stratum of the *chaebol,* moreover, comes from the privileged offspring of the old propertied classes. Finally, labor has been given limited opportunity to organize itself formally. The inequities that result from these flaws in the system tarnish the success of the ROK's developmental experience, but they remain just that, flaws in a correctable system, unlike the much more oppressive features in the North.

## U.S. Interests in the Korean Peninsula

What is frequently lost sight of in any discussion of developments on the Korean peninsula is that the regime in the South has been significantly influenced by the political democracy of the West, despite the ROK's failure to attain the ideal.

With the exception of Japan, the non-communist nations of Asia have been beset by major political, economic, and security problems since the end of World War II. These have been reflected in the emergency measures taken throughout the region. The Republic of China on Taiwan, the Philippines, Thailand, and Indonesia, among others, have invoked martial law to offset real or perceived threats. Special security regulations have been employed to protect against subversive threats in Malaysia, Singapore, Indonesia, Taiwan, and Thailand, to name only those nations of East and Southeast Asia. The ROK provides more political freedoms and civil liberties to its citizens, and immeasurably more material abundance, than do the communist systems in the DPRK, the Socialist Republic of Vietnam, and the People's Republic of China.

While Americans rightly wish to see improvements in the human rights provisions in the non-communist nations of East and Southeast Asia, direct intervention or punitive sanctions do very little to achieve that end. When Jimmy Carter's administration made human rights a U.S. foreign policy priority, the aggressive effort to compel the compliance of foreign governments created complex, unmanageable problems.[26] Few countries outside of Western Europe and Japan could meet those standards. The most grievous offenders were communist nations, over which Washington had little influence. The nations most vulnerable to U.S. pressures were the less grievous offenders with whom we often had important security and economic relations. Putting pressure, whether publicly or discretely, on these nations threatened to destabilize systems already under stress. When they did collapse, their collapse brought precious little improvement. The disappearance of the Shah from Iran ushered in the Ayatollah; the overthrow of Somoza empowered the Sandinistas—just as Lon Nol gave way to Pol Pot, Batista to Castro, and Saigon to Hanoi. In none of these instances were human rights enhanced, political democracy improved, or U.S. interests served.

Those political systems that have emulated the industrialized democracies have generally combined a democratic ideal with strategies of economic growth and industrialization predicated on a relatively free market. The coupling of free market activity and political pluralism makes good sense since evidence suggests that they are mutually supportive. To function with efficiency, a free market requires at a minimum a free flow of information. The free market creates a wide variety of interest groups. Protection of their interests requires accurate information, freedom to choose investment and mechandizing strategies, foreign contacts, mobility, and influence over government policies. All of this creates an environment hostile to central controls, which are counter-productive and ultimately dysfunctional.

In consequence, these nations—potential political democracies—will probably, in time, enhance their political and civil rights. Some have already shown just such an evolution, such as the Republic of China on Taiwan.[27] A similar case can be made for the ROK, particularly when the developments of the late 1980s are taken into account.

It is in the long-term interest of the United States that these non-communist systems prosper and evolve. Their success nourishes the democratic ideal and strengthens the forces to which the United States must appeal in its contest with its formidable socialist adversaries.

None of this means that the United States should be indifferent to derogations of political and civil rights. U.S. counsel, unobtrusive but serious, has been effective in the past. How emphatic that counsel is should be determined by a multitude of considerations, including the extent of the crises that are used to justify infractions. Different regimes are exposed to different risks. Most of the nations of Southeast Asia face insurrectionary movements that threaten not only a specific regime, but the survival of the nation itself.[28]

For the ROK, the principal threat from its inception has been the North, an enemy of significant military superiority. For four decades, the ROK has pursued its national goals in the ominous shadow of attack.

The United States has assumed obligations with respect to the survival of the ROK. Those obligations have grown out of deep moral considerations as well as realpolitik. For forty years, the United States has deployed forces in Korea in defense of democracy, and U.S. strategists have argued that a democratic ROK is critical to the defense of East Asia and a major deterrent to Soviet military misadventure.

# 4
# *External Threats*

ONCE MORE A victim of its geography, Korea was caught up in the rapidly escalating conflict between international communism and the industrial democracies at the end of World War II. The peninsula again became a strategic conduit for forces seeking expansion to the open ocean and the inlands of Japan, or for those seeking a foothold on the Asian landmass.

Before the end of the war, it was clear that the post-war period would be filled with tension and conflict, real and potential. A quarter of a century earlier, Lenin had written, "As long as capitalism and socialism exist, we cannot live in peace: in the end, one or the other will triumph." In 1948, Stalin charged that "the present leaders of the U.S.A. and Great Britain" were pursuing "a policy of aggression." The Soviets insisted that "aggressive forces" in the United States were "thirsting for new war. They need war to obtain super-profits, to plunder other countries."[1]

Mao Zedong was even more emphatic. In 1948, he argued that "since the victory of World War II, U.S. imperialism and its running dogs in various countries have taken the place of fascist Germany . . . and are frantically preparing a new world war." And in 1949, "When we say 'imperialism is ferocious,' we mean . . . that the imperialists will never lay down their butcher knives," especially the United States.[2]

By the winter of 1948, the Chinese communists had made their assessment of international relations very clear. Liu Shaoqi, then second in command of the Chinese communist party, argued that the United States was "harnessed to the chariot of eight notorious financial groups, including those of Morgan, Rockefeller, Du Pont, Mellon, etc.," who sought to "directly or indirectly enslave all the nations of the world."[3]

This quaint notion of international dynamics was supplemented by a conviction that "proletarian internationalism" required the communist nations to support other "oppressed" nations to resist the capitalist "schemes for the enslavement of the whole world" then being undertaken by "American imperialism."[4]

The communists of North Korea thus had every reason to expect substantial assistance from the Soviet Union and the Chinese communists should they ever decide to confront "American imperialism." Moreover, by the time the Chinese communist party acceded to power in Beijing, the DPRK was providing a measure of strategic defense of Chinese territory.

All this created a singular atmosphere in Pyongyang. For almost a century Koreans had sought to ensure an independent and secure future for their nation. Kim Il-sung pursued that vision through a commitment to revolutionary Marxism-Leninism, and both the Chinese communists and the Soviet Union responded favorably.

The pattern was familiar to anyone who knew something of Korea's history. Korea has often looked to foreign powers to ensure its security or assist in the attainment of some national purpose. In 1950, Kim Il-sung concluded that the time was right to reunify the peninsula and realize the long-held dream of Korean nationalism. International Marxism-Leninism was convinced that "imperialism" was in its inevitable decline. Mao Zedong and Liu Shaoqi were eloquent in their conviction that World War II was the preamble to the final resolution of the conflict between the two historic forces of capitalism and socialism. The victory of communism would usher in the "ultimate liberation of the whole of mankind as well as the ultimate liberation of all nations of the world."[5]

The ideological convictions of Marxism-Leninism played a considerable part in Kim's decision to launch the armed attack on the ROK. The invasion of South Korea would be part of that final wave of the triumphal world revolution that had begun in 1917 in czarist Russia.

The unhappy history of the Korean conflict made very clear how much more complicated the world situation was. On June 25, 1950, the DPRK launched a surprise invasion of the ROK. The following day the UN Security Council condemned the invasion as an act of aggression, demanded the withdrawal of the invading troops, and urged its members to aid South Korea. Soon thereafter, President Harry Truman authorized the use of American units in Korea, and a few days later the United Nations placed the forces of fifteen other member nations under U.S. command. At enormous cost in blood and treasure, the forces of South Korea, the United States, and the United Nations pushed the North Koreans and more than a million Chinese soldiers back beyond the border. The tense post-war began.

*Security Issues*

The Korean War defined the strategic obligations of the United States in East Asia. Prior to the attack, Washington had announced that neither Korea nor Taiwan were within the defense periphery of the United States. In fact, the possibility of an attack on South Korea was not seriously considered. The Soviet Union had suffered so grievously in World War II, and the new People's Republic of China was in such disorder, that it was deemed improbable that either would underwrite North Korean aggression.

The invasion was nevertheless launched, and the United States was compelled to deal with the issue of communist expansion. The takeover of the heartland of Europe could be rationalized as the consequence of the war against Nazi Germany, the common enemy. The communist seizure of China could be laid to the ravages of a civil war. But the invasion of South Korea by the forces from the North was quite different.

The North Korean forces, moreover, were undeniably equipped with Soviet weapons; the seven invading divisions had been trained by the Soviet occupation forces; and the 150 tanks and armored fighting vehicles that spearheaded the advance were Soviet built. The attack on the South was something more than a civil war.

A decision had to be made, and quickly. The forces of international communism could not be allowed to violate national boundaries, overthrow governments, or threaten global security.[6] Less than a week after the attack, the United States dispatched ground forces to support the beleaguered ROK troops then in full retreat, thus implementing its policy of "containment" of communist expansion in East Asia.

In due course it became evident that however bloody and prolonged the struggle, the United States would not employ nuclear weapons. In 1949, the Soviet Union had successfully detonated its first nuclear device, and any use of nuclear weapons by U.S. forces in Korea could lead to a nuclear exchange.

It also became evident that any conflict in East Asia would require massive sea-lift capabilities. During the Korean War over 5 million troops were transported by sea to the combat areas. Each soldier required four tons of ship cargo to maintain him at the level of combat efficiency. The construction of an adequate logistics infrastructure—housing, storage, and base facilities—further increased sea-lift requirements. Combat operations, moreover, depended heavily on large tankers for oil transport. Collateral support for allied troops required still more material. In thirty-seven months of combat, the United States shipped about 44 million tons of dry cargo and more than 20 million tons of oil products by sea.[7]

Finally, nearby staging areas were essential to the success of local operations. Bases in the Japanese home islands were necessary to sustain combat operations and to provide secure rear areas for air and naval support.

For Koreans, the issue involved the political future of their unhappy nation. For the United States and the industrial democracies, the conflict was part of a vast international confrontation between two hostile social and political systems.

While the Soviet Union could take credit for establishing the rule of Kim Il-sung and supporting it in its early years, it was the PRC that rescued it from ignominious defeat during the Korean conflict. The Chinese communists suffered almost a million casualties by throwing "human waves" against the superior firepower of UN forces. For its part, the Soviet Union provided the military hardware that ultimately allowed the joint communist Chinese–DPRK forces to hold along the 38th parallel—the line that now divides North and South Korea.

Sure of its security, given the two communist powers on its borders, the government in Pyongyang embarked upon its developmental program. More than 80 percent of total investment in the years between 1954 and 1956 was devoted to heavy industry, with a clear commitment to produce war materiel.[8] Both the Soviet Union and communist China underwrote a great deal of this development by grants-in-aid amounting to three-quarters of a billion dollars over a three- or four-year period.

After the failure of the Geneva conference in 1954, both Korean regimes realized that their respective survival would depend primarily on their ability to defend themselves from military attack. Both leaders persisted in their hope of unifying the divided country, but the costs involved in a military solution called into question how much support either might expect from his allies. Nonetheless, the need for self-defense and hopes of reunification argued for maintenance of military capabilities.

In 1955, Kim Il-sung announced DPRK's policy of *juche,* or self-reliance—an effort to produce and maintain, out of its own resources, a defense capability sufficient to deter attack or, failing that, to defeat an aggressor. This did not mean that Kim rejected the aid of the Soviet Union or communist China. In his first public speech extolling *juche,* Kim explained that "internationalism and patriotism are inseparably linked." To love Korea is "to love the Soviet Union and the Socialist camp, and likewise to love the Soviet Union and the Socialist camp means to love Korea."[9]

The DPRK remained dependent on the Soviet Union for its major weapon systems, and because of its proximity to the PRC, Pyongyang made every effort to please Beijing. In 1958, the last of the troops of the Chinese People's Liberation Army left the DPRK and, following two visits to Beijing, Kim Il-sung reported that Pyongyang and Beijing were in "complete agreement" on all major issues.

All of this transpired while the Soviet Union was recovering from its trauma over the death of Stalin in 1953. The Twentieth Party Congress in the Soviet Union criticized the Stalinist "cult of personality," and the fallout affected Kim's authority in Pyongyang. Kim's opponents suggested that the DPRK emulate the post-Stalin Soviet Union and regroup behind "collective leadership"; that the draconian features of the DPRK's neo-Stalinist economic system be relaxed; and that consumer industries be developed and agricultural yield be increased to improve the nation's living standards.

The resulting party struggle allowed Kim to purge his opposition. Whatever the internal strife generated by de-Stalinization, Kim Il-sung, recognizing his dependence on Soviet aid and arms sales, was careful not to express any antagonism toward Moscow. Thus, while Kim discovered more and more affinities between the DPRK and Mao's China, he maintained his efforts to placate Moscow. By the turn of the 1960s, that proved increasingly difficult.

By then, Sino-Soviet tensions had become an international scandal. The Soviet Union, moreover, had apparently been forced to retreat from confrontation with the United States over the Cuban missile crisis. In those evolving circumstances, Kim Il-sung gravitated still further toward Beijing, and consequently lost Moscow's favor.

In late 1962, at a time when the DPRK's economic and agricultural difficulties were beginning to surface, Moscow reduced its economic aid to the DPRK to a minimum. Kim Il-sung nevertheless attempted to remain friendly to Moscow through the early months of 1963, but he received little encouragement.

By the end of the year, DPRK publications were denouncing "certain persons" and a "certain party" for giving themselves over to "big power chauvinism," meddling in the affairs of others, and attempting to harness other members of the "socialist camp" to their own interests. By mid-1964, the North Koreans were openly criticizing the Soviet Union. Ever conscious of the "imperialist" armies of the South, Pyongyang drew closer to the PRC for support.

Against this background, the Korean Workers' Party adopted

the "Four Great Military Policy Lines" in 1962—to "arm the entire population," "fortify the entire country," train cadres for the military, and "modernize the entire armed forces."[10] By the middle of the decade, the DPRK had put together a system of reserves, a Worker-Peasant Red Guard, and a militia consisting of nearly all able-bodied men between the ages of eighteen and forty-five. An officer corps was also trained to allow the rapid expansion of the regular army in the event of total mobilization. Arms factories, airfield revetments, storage facilities, and communications adjuncts were constructed underground to secure against air attack. Along the demilitarized zone that separated the North from the South, a network of tunnels connected hardened artillery and rocket emplacements.

By 1965, it became apparent that only the Soviet Union could provide the advanced weapon systems and the economic support that the DPRK required. As a consequence, and with Nikita Khrushchev's loss of power in the Soviet Union, Pyongyang turned once again to Moscow.

Although the DPRK was developing the capability to manufacture a good deal of its own military equipment, between 1964 and 1973 it obtained about three-fourths of its sophisticated weapons from the Soviet Union. The PRC's major weapon systems were generally obsolescent, clearly inferior to the American systems, and probably inferior to those of the Republic of Korea.

Along with the military buildup, Kim Il-sung launched an aggressive program for the "revolutionary resolution" of the situation on the Korean peninsula—an effort to destabilize the ROK regime. Trained agents were dispatched to organize an underground revolutionary party and associated subversive front groups in the ROK. By 1968, ROK intelligence services had identified and arrested some 150 persons involved in these activities; 73 were tried and 9 executed.[11]

At the same time, the DPRK provoked incidents along the demilitarized zone (DMZ)—59 in 1965, escalating to 629 in 1968. In January 1968, moreover, a commando team from the North penetrated ROK defenses, entered Seoul, and attempted to assassinate Park Chung-hee. Later that year another special forces unit landed in the ROK in an attempt to establish a guerrilla base, recruit combatants, and orchestrate terrorist activity against the Seoul government. That same year DPRK gunboats attacked and seized the U.S. navy intelligence vessel Pueblo, and the following year, 1969, the North Koreans shot down a U.S. navy EC-121 reconnaissance aircraft, killing thirty-one Americans.

The increase in North Korean belligerency caused some concern in Moscow. The Soviets, for example, were uncommonly slow in endorsing the North Korean attack on the U.S. reconnaissance aircraft, and then only after the Soviet Union had assisted the United States in its search for survivors. Soviet reservations seemed to have some effect. The number of recorded incidents along the DMZ declined from the high of 629 in 1968 to 110 in 1969 and all but ceased by 1972.

This is not to suggest that the DPRK's military buildup had decelerated. Throughout the early 1970s, although the DPRK had a smaller economic base and a weaker productive system than the ROK, its military budget surpassed the ROK's in both percentage of GNP and in actual terms.[12] The DPRK allocated about 15 to 20 percent of its total GNP to the military.

At the same time as the Soviet Union was becoming concerned about DPRK belligerency, Beijing began to re-establish relations with Pyongyang. In 1970, Zhou Enlai visited the DPRK, the first such visit by a high-ranking PRC official since 1964.

With his confidence revived, Kim prepared to renew his aggressions against the South. In 1974, the ROK military discovered a DPRK tunnel that extended 1.2 kilometers (0.74 miles) south of the DMZ. The tunnel was large enough to allow a regiment of DPRK troops, in one hour, to jeopardize the forward defense positions of the ROK. Later that year, another attempt was made by DPRK agents to assassinate Park Chung-hee; in 1975, another tunnel was found in the Chorwon area of the DMZ; in August 1976, DPRK soldiers killed two U.S. army officers in the Joint Security Area at Panmunjom; in 1977, a U.S. helicopter was shot down after it inadvertently strayed into DPRK territory; and in 1978 several heavily armed DPRK special forces combatants landed on the ROK coast, where they killed four civilians before being killed themselves by ROK security personnel.

Throughout these years, there were many incidents at sea involving DPRK naval vessels and ROK fishing boats. Some fishing boats were sunk, with casualties among the fishermen. Ashore, the DPRK attempted to burrow ten more tunnels along the DMZ to allow its special forces to penetrate the ROK.

By the end of the 1970s, the pattern of DPRK behavior had become reasonably well established. North Korea had become a garrison state, sustaining a military establishment that consumed about 20 percent of the nation's total output, and it undertook frequent incendiary actions against the South. Its relationships with its patrons in Beijing and Moscow were good, but hedged with reservations. The Soviet Union, for instance, hesitated to provide Pyongyang with the same advanced weapon systems it supplied to its other clients. Nor had Moscow been as forthcoming as Pyongyang would like in transferring capital and technology. At the same time, the difficulties between the Soviet Union and the PRC made life uncertain for the DPRK leadership. Throughout this period—from 1953 until the end of the 1970s—the government in Seoul was burdened by the task of assuring security in the face of a complex and threatening situation.

At the end of the Korean War, the ROK had more than half a million men under arms. Equipped with U.S. weapons and trained by U.S. personnel, its military forces provided the nation with a credible defense capability. Between 1950 and the mid-1960s, the United States provided the ROK with the bulk of its military equipment. At the cost of some $2.5 billion, mostly in the form of grants, the ROK added jet fighters and fighter-bombers, artillery, tanks, destroyers, frigates, and a variety of surface-to-surface and air-to-air missiles to its inventory. Two U.S. military divisions, moreover, numbering some sixty thousand men, remained on the peninsula to serve as a counter to PRC forces stationed immediately beyond the Yalu River in Northeast China.

During the Vietnam War in the 1960s, some 300,000 ROK

troops fought alongside the Americans and the South Vietnamese. As a result, the ROK armed forces gained experience in combat and with state-of-the-art weapon systems that vastly increased their combat readiness.

By the end of the 1960s, however, the conflict in Southeast Asia had strained the resources, the patience, and the determination of the Americans to the limit. In 1969, President Richard Nixon announced his "Guam Doctrine," which affirmed that, while the United States would keep "all its treaty commitments," its security partners henceforth would be expected to "assume primary responsibility" for providing the manpower necessary for their own territorial defense.[13] This announcement was followed by Washington's decision to withdraw the U.S. Seventh Infantry Division from the Korean peninsula in 1971–1972. Most of the East Asian capitals understood the Guam Doctrine as a signal of U.S. disengagement from its commitments in the region. The predictable consequence in Seoul was great anxiety, as it faced undiminished belligerency from the North.

As a result, in the early 1970s, the ROK increased its self-defense capabilities. A military modernization program was supported by heavy investment in industrial machinery plants and defense-related industries. Beginning in 1971, defense outlays, in real terms, rose at an annual average rate of 12.5 percent. By 1975, ROK military expenditures equaled those of the DPRK.

With the total collapse of the Republic of Vietnam, the United States reconsidered the forward deployment of U.S. troops in Korea, fearing that U.S. forces might become involved in another Asian conflict. In December 1976, President-elect Jimmy Carter voiced his intention to withdraw U.S. ground forces from the ROK over phased intervals, to be completed by July 1982. The ROK, in anticipation of U.S. disengagement, had initiated a program of "Force Improvement" in 1976. It planned to purchase attack and interceptor aircraft, air-defense weapon systems, more modern armored vehicles, and anti-tank weapons. The ROK also decided to set up domestic production lines for small arms and artillery, and to construct a logistics network and storage facilities for war reserves.

More than $7.5 billion was allocated for the first phase of the plan. By the end of the decade, Seoul was spending ten times as much on defense as it had in 1976.[14] By the beginning of the 1980s, both North and South Korea had created armed forces to serve their purposes and had thereby purchased some measure of security.

## *The Military Balance*

At the end of the 1970s, the United States reconsidered its plan to withdraw its ground forces from the ROK. Many factors influenced the reversal of policy, principal among them a revised assessment of the military capabilities of the DPRK. Not only was there evidence that the DPRK ground forces numbered about 700,000 rather than the previously estimated 440,000, but the number of armored units and aircraft had been underestimated as well.

The standing forces of the DPRK military had, in fact, almost doubled between 1970 and 1980. Among its forces, about 100,000 troops were special forces: commandos, airborne and seaborne rapid deployment forces, river-fording troops, and special infiltration combatants. Some 180 Antonov An-2s could airlift troops behind ROK lines, and 90 landing craft were available for rapid river crossings and coastal assaults—all essentially geared for invasion.

DPRK heavy artillery and long-range mortars, moreover, were emplaced in hardened positions along the DMZ to provide heavy support fire for armored forces poised for a follow-up invasion. In both categories of weapon systems—artillery and armor—the DPRK had every advantage over the ROK. Its forces were equipped with self-propelled artillery and truck-mobile, 122mm multiple rocket launchers that could supply fire support for advance echelons. The ROK defenders would be caught between barrages from hardened artillery positions along the DMZ, fire from special forces, and ordnance from mobile artillery and rocket launchers along their flanks and at their rear. It was estimated that 20 percent of all ROK defenders would be eliminated in the first ninety seconds of the assault. Seoul, inhabited by 25 percent of the ROK's population and producing about 30 percent of its total GNP, is only forty kilometers (25 miles) from the DMZ. Following a standard Soviet attack routine, DPRK tanks could reach the outskirts of the city within forty-eight hours.[15]

The DPRK air force outnumbered the ROK's by a ratio of about 2:1 by the early 1980s, although it was probably inferior in quality. DPRK airfields, also located close to the DMZ, were clearly intended for surprise aircraft sorties against ROK defenders. Ground-attack aircraft would provide air support for assault troops, neutralizing strong points, interdicting supply lines, and scattering defenders.

In fact, the DPRK military forces were manifestly deployed for invasion rather than defense, while the ROK forces were as clearly entrenched for defense. If attacked, ROK forces, characterized by anti-tank defenses and hardened strong points along the principal invasion routes, could certainly give a good account of themselves, but they would be at a considerable disadvantage. The ROK air defense capabilities were hardly adequate to protect troop assembly and staging areas and storage and transport facilities. DPRK airfields are so close to the DMZ that the ROK would have very little early warning of attack. Low-flying aggressor aircraft could penetrate to the rear areas largely without detection.

The DPRK also deployed a substantial navy. Equipped by the Soviet Union, it included a large number of small craft, configured for coastal defense and amphibious assaults. The Soviet Union had transferred several Whiskey-class attack submarines to the DPRK, and the PRC handed over at least seven Soviet-designed, but Chinese-built, Romeo-class attack boats. At the end of the 1970s, the DPRK had a total of thirteen attack submarines. They could put ROK shipping at grave risk, especially since the ROK imports all its fossil fuels, essential in any modern conflict.

Along with the submarines, the DKRP had by 1978 put together a large fleet of fast attack craft, including about twenty that were missile capable. Those were supplemented by about

220 gunboats and torpedo patrol craft. These craft were not only capable of interdicting ship traffic, but could undertake incursions along the ROK coastline, land special forces, and disrupt road and rail transport as well as communications throughout the country.[16]

Finally, the DPRK was well supplied with Soviet anti-shipping mines, whereas the ROK had limited anti-mine and anti-submarine warfare capabilities.

In the event of a conflict, the DPRK had reasonable hope of success, even with the tripwire presence of about 35,000 U.S. troops along the DMZ—if the United States were occupied elsewhere and could not or would not bring its naval and air forces to the combat zone. Nonetheless, invasion of the South would be very hazardous. DPRK forces could expect to sustain grievous losses in the fight to break through hardened strong points along the invasion routes.

For the ROK defenders, the question remains whether the DPRK leadership will embark on such a risky enterprise. Anticipating the military behavior of the DPRK is complicated by the fact that policy decisions are made in a manner that defies normal cost accounting.

The DPRK leadership has undertaken dangerous provocations in the past, including terrorist assaults, assassinations, special service and commando raids against civilians, and armed attacks on U.S. naval vessels and aircraft. These provocations continued into the 1980s with the bombing in Rangoon—the assassination of the ROK deputy prime minister, foreign minister, and general secretary for economic affairs. This bombing, which killed and maimed dozens, provided chilling insight into the peculiar cost calculus employed by the DPRK authorities. The Burmese official report called it a planned attack carried out by DPRK commandos to destabilize the ROK government.[17] This atrocity was followed by the inflight bombing of an ROK passenger airliner by DPRK agents.

The ROK leadership is therefore legitimately preoccupied with the military buildup in the North, and with the intentions behind the buildup.

The man who dominates the DPRK has been described as the

"ever-victorious iron-willed brilliant commander" whose "exploits will continue to shine for a thousand years, for ten thousand years, lighting the world of posterity." He had identified his "supreme national task" as "liberating the South Korean people and unifying the fatherland." And there are repeated broadcasts proclaiming that "the guidance of Kim Il-sung" is "invincible" and capable of performing "superhuman miracles everywhere."[18] Kim Il-sung, in his dotage, might yet embark on a military adventure to achieve the "supreme national task" before his death. Little wonder the ROK leadership is troubled.

The DPRK has entered a critical period as the aged Kim Il-sung reaches the end of his life. Although he has groomed his son Kim Jong-il—the "Dear Leader"—as his successor, the junior Kim's assumption of power is not certain, since the military may not support the succession. The military may, in fact, feel that reunification should be undertaken soon, while Kim Il-sung is still in power, or on the occasion of his death.

The DPRK military, by the end of the 1980s, had increased its in-service personnel to about 838,000 with a very high percentage serving as armed combatants. The three thousand tanks and assault guns in service include the Soviet T-62 and T-72 battle tanks, and there are more than one thousand armored personnel carriers and thousands of trucks. Firepower in the field has been increased by the addition of more large-caliber artillery pieces, mortars, and howitzers, and there are about two thousand truck-mobile, 122mm multiple rocket launchers. Frog 5 and Frog 7 surface-to-surface missiles have recently been supplemented by Soviet SCUD missiles.

The airlift capacity of the DPRK has been improved by the addition of about 100 more An-2 aircraft, providing a fleet of some 280 transport craft. The DPRK has also acquired about 20 Mi-4 and 50 Mi-8 transport helicopters capable of the rapid airlift of about 1,500 fully armed troops, and about 80 Hughes 500-C helicopters have been bought from West Germany.

The most dramatic improvement has been in the DPRK's air force. MiG-27s and MiG-29 Fulcrums—the most advanced interceptor/fighter in Soviet service—have been sighted on DPRK airfields.

The DPRK forces have also acquired the Mi-24 Hind, a rotary-wing flying assault weapon that serves as a platform for formidable firepower and can carry a dozen armed combatants. Gatling guns, guided missiles, and unguided rockets in pods mounted on the Hind can respond to almost any contingency. The Hind's kill-to-loss ration against tanks has been reported to be 12:1 (in some sources 19:1).[19]

In short, the armed forces of the DPRK are modern, mobile, and formidable. North Korea deploys delivery systems that threaten ROK defenses, military targets, ports, and metropolitan areas, and it has developed chemical warfare capabilities. In fact, the DPRK has the fifth largest armed force in the world.[20]

While the defense expenditures of the government in Seoul now exceed, in real terms, those of the North, the ROK defense is predicated on the immediate involvement of the U.S. military should an attack occur. To repel a DPRK invasion, not only would U.S. fighter and fighter-bombers stationed in the ROK be needed, but also massive air strikes by B-52 bombers based in Guam as well as tactical air support from U.S. units in Japan and the Philippine archipelago. And all this requires that U.S. forces be immediately available.

The political instability in the ROK, moreover, compares unfavorably with the iron discipline in the DPRK—one more enticement to aggression. The ROK is further weakened by its growing trade friction with the United States. Some Americans, as a result, have suggested that the United States distance itself from the ROK and withdraw its ground forces.

Should that happen, the DPRK leadership would have achieved one of its principal foreign policy goals, with ominous implications not only for the future of the Republic of Korea, but for the security interests of the United States as well.

*The Broader Security Context*

During the past two decades, the Soviet Union pursued a military buildup unparalleled in history. Since at least 1969, the Soviet Union has invested more, in real terms, in military expenditures than the United States. While U.S. military spending declined at an average annual rate of about 2 percent between 1972 and 1981, that of the Soviet Union steadily increased. Even with the increases introduced by the Reagan administration, U.S. military expenditure consumed no more than about 6.2 percent of the nation's GNP compared to the estimated 15 to 20 percent of GNP of the Soviet Union.[21]

Back in 1960, the United States enjoyed general military superiority, but by 1980, the global military balance had undergone significant change. In the intervening years, economic, military, political, and social problems impeded Washington from implementing a coherent defense program. U.S. policies were interpreted as efforts to reduce America's overseas commitments; for example, the Guam Doctrine that reduced U.S. ground forces in East Asia, the withdrawal of the 7th Division from Korea, and Washington's readiness to downgrade relations with its long-time ally on Taiwan.

For its part, the Soviet Union, because of increasing tensions with the PRC, began a program of military enhancement in East Asia in the mid-1960s that saw the deployment of fifty-six motorized infantry, armor, artillery, and support divisions in the Siberian, Transbaikal, and Far East military districts along the 7,000 kilometer border with the PRC.[22] The Soviet strategic weapons are capable of targeting all major objectives in East Asia, from the Japanese home islands to Australia.

Soviet forces in East Asia are now supplied with the most advanced weapon systems. The Pacific fleet, moreover, is today the largest of the Soviet fleets, deploying some 295 large surface vessels, including 90 attack boats, and about 120 submarines.[23] Coupled with long-range bombers, they threaten the sea-lanes essential to U.S. and U.S.-allied forces in East Asia.

In 1950, when North Korea invaded the South, U.S. forces controlled the air over the combat zone and the sea-lanes in the immediate vicinity. The decisive landings at Inchon that turned the tide of the war would have otherwise been impossible.

By the 1980s, all that had changed. The United States had lost every advantage it had enjoyed in East Asia since the end of World War II. The Soviet Union's new capabilities dramatically changed the military balance in the area. As though to signal the extent of the changes, General Secretary Mikhail Gorbachev announced a new and ambitious Soviet policy for East Asia in a speech at Vladivostok in July 1986.

Although Gorbachev's speech emphasized economic and diplomatic considerations, he nonetheless made it clear that security remained a critical concern. Gorbachev spoke of "establishing a comprehensive system of international security," the system proposed by the Soviet Union. Gorbachev also spoke of the enemy, "the ruling forces of imperialism" that are "blinded by animosity towards socialism, by imperial ambitions or close links with the war business." More specifically, the enemy was "the militarized triangle of Washington, Tokyo, and Seoul" set up as a consequence of "the pressure of the U.S.A."[24]

For Gorbachev, moreover, reunification of the peninsula would follow the "reasonable" prescriptions of Kim Il-sung: the withdrawal of U.S. forces; the elimination of constraints on communist activities in the South; the suppression of "fascist elements" in the South that are opposed to "democracy"; and the establishment of a "confederal political system" on the peninsula that would receive "the active support and encouragement of progressive people the world over."[25] In effect, a communist-dominated Korea.

That would probably result in the withdrawal of the ROK from U.S. security arrangements in East Asia, which could be catastrophic. Ichiji Sugita, former chief of staff of the Japanese Ground Self-Defense Force, has insisted that if the Korean peninsula should fall to hostile forces, the security of Japan would be grievously compromised.[26]

For the United States, the loss of the ROK as an ally would create a number of problems, not the least of which would be a reduced capacity to seal the Tsushima Strait—one of the three major waterways used by the Soviets to reach the open Pacific from the inland waters of Northeast Asia. The loss of U.S. air bases and naval facilities in the ROK would also impair our ability to contain a Soviet breakout through the strait in time of conflict, or to interdict Soviet resupply to inland water bases in the event of protracted conventional warfare.

The Soviet Union has only recently altered its policies to reflect the importance of the DPRK. In the past, Moscow refused to underwrite Kim Il-sung's belligerency, fearing it might involve the Soviet Union in a conflict in East Asia before it had effective defensive and offensive capabilities in the region.

Since Kim Il-sung's visit to Moscow in 1984, however, the DPRK leadership has resigned itself to the fact that it must rely on the Soviet Union for most of its oil supplies, a quarter of its total trade turnover, and almost all of its advanced weaponry. After Kim's visit, Pyongyang emphasized the importance of "proletarian internationalism," Moscow's code phrase for loyalty to its foreign policy.

More important, perhaps, than the transfer of Soviet weapon systems is that for the first time the armed forces of the Soviet Union and the DPRK have undertaken joint military exercises. In October 1986, for example, DPRK joint naval exercises were conducted off the coast of North Korea.

The Soviet Union has apparently gained supply and servicing rights in Nampo, on the western coast of North Korea, as well as at the port of Najin on the east coast. These ports are connected with the Soviet Union by rail and permit the Soviet navy greater flexibility.[27] As part of the same military arrangements, Soviet aircraft now regularly overfly DPRK territory on their way to bases in Southeast Asia. This has been accompanied by an increase in North Korean air activity throughout the area.

It is not known why the Soviet Union changed its policy with respect to providing advanced weapons to the DPRK, or why it has intensified its military cooperation with Pyongyang. At a minimum, the changes would seem to be a function of the changed military balance in Northeast Asia.

Since 1980, the People's Republic of China has become increasingly neutral. In 1981, after trying for some time to convince the industrialized democracies to join in a "united front" against the Soviet Union, Beijing announced a policy of "independence," a desire to be free from any alliance. The PRC leadership proceeded to seek accommodation with the Soviet Union, greatly reducing its hostility toward what it used to call Soviet social fascism and betrayal of Marxism-Leninism.[28]

Beijing also slowed its military modernization. Allocations for the military fell by about 30 percent in real terms between 1980 and 1985. The Chinese People's Liberation Army has been reduced by about one million members and the popular militia has been all but abandoned.

In sum, the situation in Northeast Asia has undergone significant change in the 1980s. The Soviets no longer talk of a Washington-Tokyo-Beijing "threat to peace." It has become a Washington-Tokyo-Seoul threat. The result is a major change in Soviet policy.

Current Soviet policy seeks to neutralize the ROK. By providing the DPRK with more modern military equipment and with substantial military cooperation, Moscow has increased the ROK's financial burden and made it more hazardous and difficult for Seoul to remain an active member of the U.S.-Japanese defense alliance.

Given the circumstances—an arms race with the North that consumes more and more of its resources, mounting trade friction with its security partners, the recurrent threat that the United States may withdraw its ground forces from the peninsula, the growing power and determination of the Soviet Union to influence developments in the region—the political leadership in Seoul has sought to reduce the risks. It has tried to "normalize" relations with Moscow. It has reopened the "dialogue" with the North. It has welcomed trade and other contacts with Beijing. And it has allowed advocates of "neutralization" and "nonalignment" to be heard in Seoul.

As for the DPRK, at the meeting of the Sixth Congress of the Korean Workers' Party in Pyongyang in October 1980, Kim Il-sung advocated the establishment of a "neutral" and "nonaligned" Korea, an initiative intended to stimulate just such an interest in the ROK.[29]

At its best, this neutrality would help realize one of the major goals of Soviet foreign policy in East Asia: the withdrawal of U.S. forward-based forces. Of course, the Soviet Union would remain as a permanent presence in the region.

The DPRK would also, of course, profit from any withdrawal of U.S. forces. Most analysts agree that "there is no reason to suppose that Pyongyang has abandoned its ultimate goal of dominating South Korea in a reunified communist Korea but, for the moment, it is engaging in more flexible tactics."[30]

At present, the United States is increasingly disadvantaged. Political and economic pressures ensure that U.S. defense expenditures will suffer major reductions well into the 1990s. There is, however, no hard evidence of corresponding reductions in Soviet military expenditures.[31] The trends in East Asia appear to be moving against the United States; everything favors a continuation of Moscow's present policies.

Recently Americans were reminded that

> The two key variables in the Korean problem remain the American commitment to South Korea and political stability in the South. If the United States were to withdraw its troops from South Korea, an entirely new and unstable situation could be created on the peninsula. If the Russians and North Koreans were to come to the conclusion that the American commitment to Korea is not credible, one or the other party might well be inclined to take much greater risks in order to dominate the southern part of the peninsula.
>
> A protracted period of political instability in South Korea might also encourage the North toward adventurism.[32]

At present, the Republic of Korea may indeed be facing a period of political instability. Should this be the case, even a firm commitment by the United States to the defense of the republic may not be sufficient to ensure its future.

# 5
# *The Outlook*

THE 1990S WILL probably be a critical period of transition for the Korean peninsula. The Democratic People's Republic of Korea, given Kim Il-sung's age and questionable health, will soon face a major crisis of succession, and his son, the "Dear Leader," will certainly encounter opposition to his bid for power. Despite the scarcity of information from the DPRK about dissident factions, past experience shows that succession in totalitarian systems engenders serious dislocations—witness the periods following the deaths of Stalin and Mao Zedong.

The rigid system in the DPRK, with its extensive disabilities and malfunctions, calls for massive reform. North Koreans are becoming increasingly aware of the significant differences between the two peninsular political and economic systems. By the beginning of the 1990s, the GNP of the Republic of Korea will probably exceed $100 billion and per capita income will probably be above $4,500. Current estimates of the DPRK's economic growth rate for the foreseeable future range from about 3 percent, at best, to almost zero at worst.[1] Given its estimated 2.6 percent annual rate of population growth, a significant deterioration of living standards can be expected.[2]

Those differences will not only create internal tensions and hinder a smooth succession, but will make it difficult for Pyongyang to maintain its large and expensive military establishment—unless the Soviet Union is prepared to underwrite the DPRK's requirements. That is unlikely, since Moscow is facing budgetary constraints of its own.[3]

The little hard data available suggests that the DPRK faces

serious internal problems that time can only exacerbate. After having sacrificed economic concerns for a quarter of a century in pursuit of military superiority, Pyongyang may well have failed. If so, it will have failed because of still more basic failures. Economic inefficiencies will have produced cascade effects that impair the community's ability to solve any number of problems. Instability and pressures for change can hardly be gainsaid.

The next decade will be no less difficult for the ROK. One of the principal issues that will tax its management skills is the demand for political democracy—determining the pace of change and what factors should influence that pace.[4]

For most Americans, "political development"—efficacy through differentiation and equality of opportunity—necessarily means "democracy." Democracy, as we understand it, includes formal opposition parties, competitive elections, and protection of civil and political rights. Most Americans also believe that protected rights afford equality of opportunity, that democratic institutions nurture efficiency, that freedom of expression and competitive elections put a premium on successful performance, and finally, that today's complex and demanding environment requires differentiation.

To construe "political development" in some such fashion is reasonable. And Americans tend to view the election of Roh Tae-woo to the presidency of the ROK as making a positive contribution to that process. In December 1987, for the first time in its brief and troubled history, the ROK witnessed the peaceful and constitutional transfer of political power from one chief executive to another—a significant advance in political development and the realization of democracy.

There is little question about the development of the ROK's economic system. Most of the criticism turns on political development, specifically on the issue of civil and political rights. Many analysts contend that conditions in the ROK have matured to the point where demands for political democracy are reasonable and must therefore be accommodated.

This in turn will depend on a number of factors. For example, the rapidly changing economy has produced demographic changes that influence political development and that the leadership can neglect only at considerable risk.

*Demographic Changes*

Like all communities undergoing rapid economic growth and industrial development, the Republic of Korea has experienced radical changes in the size, character, and distribution of its population. Between 1954 and 1985, the ROK population more than doubled, from little more than 19 million to about 40 million, and it was transformed from an essentially rural to a largely urban population. In 1945, only 14.5 percent of the population was urban; in 1980, 57.2 percent was urban.[5] By the end of the 1970s, one out of five South Koreans was changing his residence each year. Population mobility and urban relocation have brought instability and an increasing desire for, and tolerance of, change.

At the same time, the average annual rate of growth in per capita gross national product was 8 percent, and the per capita GNP increased from about $70 in 1950 to about $3,000 in 1985. Between 1960 and 1980, literacy increased from 71 to 93 percent of the adult population. The number of persons enrolled in institutions of higher education rose from 5 to 12 percent of the total college age group during the same period. Rapid urbanization and the increase in educational opportunity resulted in the geographic concentration of intellectuals. As early as 1960, over 70 percent of all college graduates lived in cities with more than 50,000 inhabitants, even though those cities contained only 28 percent of the total population at the time.[6] Most students, though originally from the country, became residents in urbanized and increasingly sophisticated communities.

By the mid-1980s, the ROK population had become substantially more middle class in character due to the steady rise in family income, increased availability of higher education, and greater access to information. At the same time, Christianity made dramatic inroads. In 1955, about 5 percent of the population professed the Christian faith, but by the mid-1980s about 23 percent identified themselves as "believers."[7] Combined with the proliferation and differentiation of groups—professional, managerial, entrepreneurial, labor, and special interest—these demographic changes have created a very complex political environment.

For the most part, these groups represent corporate interests, and they negotiate for benefits in a political arena that has become increasingly open and permissive over the past several years. Although the beginning of the administration of Chun Doo-hwan was inauspicious, Chun eventually introduced a set of liberalizing reforms, including the lifting of a decades-long midnight curfew, the easing of restrictions on travel overseas, the restoration of political rights to many people previously barred from political activities, and a degree of campus autonomy that allowed university administrators to deal with all university affairs without interference from the Ministry of Education. As a result, university students were allowed to organize a National Federation of Student Associations, which created a support network for their political activities.

The reduction of controls over the rights of association and expression has inspired tumultuous political activity. Labor organizations, church groups, and student activists have become increasingly aggressive. The organized opposition to the Chun administration was very successful in the February 1985 National Assembly elections. Representatives of various opposition parties won the majority of the contests, and the Democratic Justice Party, the party of Chun Doo-hwan, was left without full control of the legislature.

Political activity dominated the ROK throughout 1986 and 1987. The political opposition organized into new political parties, with Kim Young-sam founding the Reunification Democratic Party and Kim Dae-jung the Party for Peace and Democracy.

During this time student activists engaged in the politics of "contestation," the disruptive politics of the streets. Between 1978 and 1986, the percentage of political prisoners in the ROK identified as students rose from 35 to 83 percent of the total. In fact, by the early 1980s, student activists had taken control of the protest movement.[8]

The first anti-American demonstrations also took place in the early 1980s. By the spring of 1984, student activists were meeting with workers to give greater force to their demands. The students identified the incumbents in government as "fascists" and the leaders of industry as "capitalists" in the service of "imperialism." The American cultural center in Pusan was burned, and the Chun government was condemned as a U.S. puppet and a "lunatic dictatorship."[9]

In June 1987, when Roh Tae-woo, then the presidential candidate of the Democratic Justice Party, announced a "democratic reform" program in anticipation of the upcoming December elections, a series of unprecedented labor disturbances followed. In fact, more than three thousand strikes were recorded over the space of three months. Many people, including those sympathetic to workers' grievances, considered them a threat to the competitiveness of ROK exports in an increasingly inhospitable international market.

In the December 1987 presidential election, the governing party's candidate—Roh Tae-woo—emerged the victor with a plurality of 36.6 percent of the votes cast. Kim Young-sam received 28 percent and Kim Dae-jung 27 percent. Almost 90 percent of the eligible voters had cast their ballots. Opposition charges of fraud and government interference in the election were not supported by U.S. observers. For example, Stephen Solarz, chairman of the Subcommittee on Asian and Pacific Affairs of the House Foreign Affairs Committee, reported little evidence of fraud.

By this time, the ROK had embarked on a course to satisfy the democratic aspirations of its population. This effort was triggered, in part, by a concern for the success of the International Olympic Games to be hosted in Seoul in the summer of 1988. The government sought to avoid any confrontation that might tarnish its public image. But this effort goes beyond concern; it is the consequence of fundamental changes in the political character of the ROK population.

Unlike the hegemonic system in the North, the political system in the South has responded to changes that have attended its economic growth and industrialization. In the ROK, the legitimation of political rule—however much removed from the ideal—is perceived to rest on the support of the people. The ROK people have accepted emergency regulations but they have persisted in their expectation that, one day, the government would satisfy their democratic aspirations.

Throughout the history of the republic a formal opposition has always been tolerated and public demonstrations of dissent, however circumscribed, have always been possible. The result has been a history of political conflict and instability, in stark contrast to the oppression and rigidity of the North. There has been diversity and competition in the ROK because the government did not and could not control all the emerging status groups, corporate bodies, and special interests. The increasing complexity of occupational roles and lifestyles is expressed in diversity of opinion and expression, and in an increasing demand for the protection of civil and political rights.[10]

A great many factors will influence progress toward full democratization in the ROK; among the most important is the proliferation of corporate interest groups.

*Major Political Actors*

Like most developing countries, the Republic of Korea maintains a military establishment that has and does exercise significant, and at times determinant, political influence. In 1953, after the Korean War, the ROK possessed a powerful military, a corporate entity that enjoyed a monopoly of force, a capacity for rapid communication and mobility, and an institutional discipline—all that was needed for political dominance.[11]

Military regimes in many developing countries are similar in character. In the ROK the persistence of a major external threat increased the importance of the military, which continues as a major force in ROK politics and will probably remain so in the future.

In the recent past, however, the military has been increasingly reluctant to involve itself directly in domestic politics. Even though the Chun Doo-hwan administration was severely taxed by dissidence in 1986 and 1987, the military resisted the suggestion that it assume emergency rule. It is becoming more professional and less disposed to play a political role.

A body of big-business interests has also enjoyed major influence in the ROK. By 1983, the *chaebol*—the large industrial conglomerates—were producing much of the nation's gross industrial output and 70 percent of South Korea's exports. As a result, especially with the ROK's export-oriented strategy, they were of critical importance to the government and were politically very influential.

The Chun Doo-hwan administration favored the large corporate institutions, providing them funding and privileged access to loans. The economic success of the republic continues to rest, in large part, with the *chaebol,* whose spokesmen exercise political influence through the Federation of Economic Organizations and Korean Industries as well as through a number of collateral informal channels.

Small- and medium-sized industries (SMI), in turn, are represented by the Korea Chamber of Commerce and the Federation of Korean Medium and Small Businesses, which have enjoyed little special advantage in the past. In general, industrial progress and export growth rely on economies of scale. Small- and medium-sized industries contribute to the process, but are not well represented in those limited areas where growth is concentrated.

As a consequence, SMIs tend to be neglected and only marginally profitable. Some estimates indicate that as many as 90 percent of the SMIs have poor viability. Several institutions were created to provide capital for SMIs, but they have had little success and thus enjoy relatively meager political influence.[12]

Within the context of the general industrial community, organized labor constitutes yet another important interest group. In the past, government controls fostered company or enterprise unions, to the exclusion of trade or industrial unions. In consequence, labor was relatively ineffective in politics. The real and fancied inequities that resulted fueled the major 1987 labor unrest.

In the countryside, the farm community represents still another politically important interest group. The rural community has provided the government a substantial part of its political base. Both the Park and Chun administrations depended on the rural vote for support. In turn, the government provided protective tariffs on agricultural imports and subventions for farm produce in an effort to maintain family farm incomes.

In the elections of December 1987, Roh Tae-woo won a large plurality of votes in the rural areas. In the metropolitan Seoul election district, he came in third, behind Kim Young-sam and Kim Dae-jung, but he won a plurality of votes in metropolitan Pusan, Taegu, and Inchon. In other words, the government showed strength not only in the rural areas, but among the urban middle class as well.

The broad middle class includes entrepreneurs of small- and medium-sized industries, professionals, skilled workers, merchants, and the self-employed. It harbors a general concern for democratic rights, economic stability, political order, and national security.

Whatever their objective condition, 60 to 70 percent of all South Koreans identify themselves as "middle class." This includes many urban wage workers, who tend to share the conservative, democratic sentiments of that class.

The middle class sustains the pressure for democratic change, but other groups in the ROK are not so committed to change—those who have profited from the controls of the past and those who urge radical changes that would impair "bourgeois democracy." It is unclear, for example, how fully the military elite identify with middle-class democratic aspirations. The industrial elite, for its part, have reservations about rapid political change, for the *chaebol* have benefited from the prevailing system.

At the other end of the spectrum, on the farthest margin of the "progressive" middle class, are the radicals. Among them is a small minority of university students. Since 1980, they have become increasingly Marxist in inspiration and increasingly anti-American in expression. They served as a catalyst for much of the violence of 1986 and 1987. Some academics and a number of foreign and domestic clerics are associated with them.

To date, none of these marginal radical groups commands mass organizations or represents substantial constituencies. Although they speak of representing the "masses," they have not succeeded in mobilizing workers, "peasants," or the urban poor. Their high visibility is probably the result of mismanagement of their protests by the government.

These, then, are the major actors in the political environment of South Korea. Together they will determine the future of the republic, but how they will do that is difficult to predict.

*Dynamics of Change*

In May of 1985, a survey was conducted in the ROK to determine the prevailing public sentiment concerning the incumbent administration. Of the more than one thousand respondents, 65.2 percent, including 60.7 percent of those of above average income, were dissatisfied with the government. In 1987, a survey indicated that 85.7 percent of those interviewed felt that the protection of civil and political rights should take priority over economic growth. Over 80 percent supported political reforms to promote democracy.[13]

It was evident, by the end of the 1980s, that the majority of citizens wanted a more democratic society. When Roh Tae-woo called for direct elections in June 1987, he was responding to widespread demand. The authorities could no longer temporize.

The presidential election of December 1987 indicated the fragility of the republic's political future—opposition candidates won 55 percent of the popular vote. Furthermore, the government party failed to win a majority in the National Assembly elections of April 1988, capturing only 125 of the 299 contested seats. The ruling party had lost its majority in the National Assembly. Allied to conservative forces, with a cabinet half composed of representatives of the preceding administration, the new president, Roh Tae-woo, will have to pursue orderly and incremental change under less than auspicious conditions.

Since his inauguration on February 25, 1988, and the establishment of the Sixth Republic, Roh Tae-woo has lifted the controls over the print and broadcast media and reduced those over educational institutions. The government has urged the new labor unions and management to resolve disputes without official intervention in order to foster differentiation and institutional pluralism.

Democratization has proceeded apace, setting forces in motion that will change the character of the ROK. The effectiveness of labor organizations will have an impact on the comparative advantage enjoyed by ROK commodities on the world market. In the past, wages have not been negotiated, but have been tied to increases in labor productivity. That will no longer be the case. The most recent spate of wage increases, following the surge of labor unrest in 1987 and 1988, point to the future. The Korea Development Institute estimates that wage increases, all other things remaining equal, can significantly impair the ROK's international competitiveness.

Things, of course, will not remain equal. There will be strong incentives for the large conglomerates to move into the manufacture of up-market products—like consumer electronics—where more profit can be made, as well as to abandon simple assembly and labor-intensive production. Where possible, large-scale producers will reduce labor costs by mechanizing the production process.

The immediate consequences will probably include at least a temporary increase in unemployment, which at present hovers around 3 to 4 percent, and, because of greater demand for investment capital, an increase in the already excessive debt-to-equity ratio that burdens heavy industry.

On the other hand, labor-saving devices will probably stimulate production in the domestic intermediate goods and machine industries. The abandonment of light commodity production by the large-scale export industries, moreover, will create market opportunities for the small- and medium-sized industries. Under less pressure from labor organizations, they can fill the domestic and foreign markets vacated by the large producers. The larger of the SMIs have already begun to make inroads in the export market and to produce some down-market items. They may well become integrated into a system of subcontracting to the larger firms, much as in the Japanese fashion.

Such changes could result in more middle-class support for gradual, if substantive, political change. The large conglomerates would feel less threatened by organized labor, and those who benefited from the gains of the small- and medium-sized industries would be less anxious to destabilize the society.

Workers, in general, would participate more effectively in larger establishments where they could better organize and press their demands. Wages would improve and increase domestic demand, to everyone's benefit.

Selling more products domestically, moreover, is one way of reducing dependence on foreign markets. Coupled with a diversification of markets, that would offset the pressure on ROK industry to reduce its trade surpluses with its major trading partners.

To institute these changes, government intervention should be fastidious and non-intrusive—more in the form of advice than compulsion. SMIs must have adequate access to finance as well as managerial and technical advice, none of which is presently available. At the end of the 1970s, for instance, a World Bank inspection team indicated that technical support was provided by the extension service of the ROK government to just 788 out of over 30,000 SMI enterprises.[14]

Given their remarkable performance in 1986 and 1987, industries of all sizes should weather the future changes. In 1986, GNP growth in the ROK was 12.5 percent, and 1987 was equally spectacular. Moreover, although there were intensive efforts by dissidents to "radicalize" labor, ROK workers are evidently more interested in economic than in political issues.[15]

With proper support, the SMIs should experience good growth. According to current estimates, by the early 1990s they could account for 45 percent of commodity exports. If that growth could be coupled with their expansion into the rural areas, it might help solve a burdensome problem.

Since most of South Korea's industries are located in metropolitan areas—Seoul, Pusan, and Taegu—little off-farm employment is available to rural populations. Thus, in 1981, 67 percent of all farm family income derived from agriculture, supplemented by funds—almost 20 percent of total farm income—from relatives living in cities. In other words, the rural population is largely dependent on farm income, and on government subsidies of farm products, for survival.[16] In return, the government receives consistent rural support, and depends on it to maintain its stability. To withdraw price supports from farm produce, or to open the domestic market to agricultural imports, would threaten political incumbents.

The spread of small- and medium-sized industry into the rural areas would provide farm families with off-farm employment and reduce their dependence on government subsidies. It would also allow the government to liberalize its policies governing agricultural imports, thus reducing trade friction with the United States.

Expanding industry into the countryside, of course, would involve great investment in rural infrastructure and social overhead. New energy sources and the expansion of rural roads and rail transport would be costly, but it would also vastly improve the quality of farm life.

With skill and some good fortune, the ROK political leadership should be able to make these economic changes without too much political instability, since the major population groups are at least minimally satisfied economically. And political rights could be expanded without courting major difficulties. The more conservative groups would respond to the orderliness and continuity of the processes, and the less fortunate would gain better access to income streams, enjoy better protection for their civil and political rights, and be better represented in general.

Barring major international dislocation, the ROK should be able to manage the major transition to a more sophisticated industrial economy and a more diversified agricultural base. In the present political situation, the executive branch must accommodate a legislature dominated by an articulate and determined opposition. This will help develop the political skills of compromise and collaboration. While political decisions will be more difficult to make and more time-consuming to implement, they will probably involve greater public participation and represent a broader democratic consensus.

In general, the political opposition in the ROK has been responsible and its criticisms constructive. While there has been a tendency to exaggerate the flaws in the republic's spectacular economic development, there has been remarkably little overt appeal to radical sentiments.[17] Involvement in the responsibilities of power will foster the management skills necessary for democratic negotiation.

There are, however, other forces operating in the ROK that are intentionally and potentially catastrophic. They can work mischief in this sensitive political environment.

*Major Threats to Democratization*

The ROK has a significant number of young people who are partially educated, frequently unemployable, and almost always alienated. Some join the radical and revolutionary cause. These student radicals are often described as "idealistic" and "romantic," when they give every appearance of being irresponsible and superficial.

In the years immediately following the founding of the republic, students frequently served as the conscience of the nation. In 1960, when Syngman Rhee violated the most elementary political precepts, students gave public voice to the unexpressed anger of outraged citizens. When they were joined by the urban middle classes, the regime could no longer rule.

If effect, students have served as a catalyst in the ROK's political life. Although those who qualify as "radical" are no more than 1 or 2 percent of the active student body at any given time, they have influence greatly disproportionate to their numbers, particularly when backed by professionals in the academic community and some few representatives of Christian denominations.

Students have many advantages as political activists. They are energetic, trained as symbol manipulators, and have little sense of adult responsibilities.[18] Only recently separated from their traditional rural roots, the unguided students are often susceptible to novel radical and countercultural influences.

After 1980, student activists in the ROK became increasingly enamored of neo-Marxist theories. The autonomy of campus life allowed student activists to organize nationally and to use confrontation as a means to "social revolution" and the political reunification of the peninsula.

With broader opportunity on the university campuses, more and more political activists were elected as leaders of student government organizations. In 1985, they set up "The Struggle Committee for the Liberation of the Masses, the Attainment of Democracy, and the Unification of the Nation," which was committed to "raising the consciousness of the masses to economic injustice," orchestrating violent attacks on American and "imperialist" targets, and marshalling street demonstrations against the American military presence and the "fascist" government.

These were the activists who occupied the Seoul offices of the United States Information Service in May 1985. The United States was charged with complicity in the "oppressions" carried out by the incumbent "military dictatorship," and was accused of "economic exploitation" and of keeping the peninsula divided by its "paranoid" anti-communist foreign policy. The following August, students attempted to invade the U.S. Embassy in Seoul, and in November, a student occupied the U.S. Chamber of Commerce office in the city. At the same time, the offices of the Democratic Justice Party Training Institute and of the chairman of the Federation of Industries were seized in the struggle against "fascism" and "imperialism."[19]

By 1985, "most student activists subscribed to the view that the United States was primarily responsible for the very existence of the military-authoritarian regime" in the ROK.[20] A year later, they were actively working to "drive U.S. imperialism" out of Korea, foment a "national democratic revolution," and pursue the unification of North and South Korea.

Throughout, student radicals attempted to mobilize labor in the service of the revolution. An estimated 1,500 student activists sought employment in industry to raise the consciousness of the "oppressed working class," while other student radicals fanned out into the countryside offering voluntary labor to farmers during the busy summer months in order to give political instructions to the "oppressed peasantry." None of this came to very much. By the middle of 1987, neither the rural nor the urban "masses" had responded to the student-inspired call to social revolution.

The fact remains that the ROK provides very little combustible material to fuel revolutionary initiatives. Between 1965 and

1980, for example, the incidence of poverty declined from 40.9 percent to 9.8 percent. Radical rhetoric to the contrary, the ROK ranks high in economic equality, even when compared with the United States and other industrially developed countries.[21]

In view of this, students can expect to receive little support for revolution from major population sectors, without which they can accomplish little.[22] When, on the other hand, student activists did receive the support of the urban middle class during the disturbances of June 1987, they were able to influence the government to permit the direct election of the president of the republic. The middle class, in effect, would support the effort to expand democratic rights, but would not back a social revolution.

Student violence based on radical ideas has thus become increasingly counterproductive. Representatives of both the Protestant and Catholic communities have pleaded with student activists to abandon "left-leaning radical ideology and the cry of . . . revolution."[23] There remains, of course, a minority of radical theologians whose *Minjung* or "people's theology" is the Korean variant of "liberation theology"—a body of notions that sees "international capitalism" as the irredeemable enemy of the "masses." Their anti-capitalist and socialist rhetoric has fed student radicalism and been at least partially responsible for the violence in the students' confrontation with authorities.[24]

More often than not, however, the Christian churches in the ROK have spoken for the democratic aspirations of the population.[25] Many church leaders, in defense of democracy, have argued that student radicalism often results from heavy-handed repression by the authorities. In some cases, students have been subjected to brutality and abuse. The cycle of wanton repression and mindless violence that resulted only contributed further to the afflictions of the nation.

Nevertheless, although student radicalism has been largely neutralized by its own failures and by the successes of democratization, under certain conditions it still could threaten the future of the republic.

Another potential threat to the realization of full democracy lies at the other end of the spectrum—the military. Military leaders have staffed the authoritarianism of the past. In the more recent past, however, the military, and their representatives who have served in the government, have been reluctant to use martial force either to remain in power or to maintain stability in the republic. As mentioned above, when there was a question of military intervention in mid-1987, the military's own assessment, the disapproval of Washington, and the democratic disposition of the middle class counseled against it. Roh Tae-woo chose compromise and negotiation rather than repression, with political democracy the beneficiary.

It is hard to imagine what might compel the military, once again, to intervene in public affairs. Although that remains a possibility, it would require a crisis of major proportions. ROK society has become so complex, consisting of various economic components, professional groups, social elements, and lifestyle communities, that the military would find it difficult to return to the political authoritarianism of the past. Such a crisis would probably not arise from internal political tensions but, more likely, from external aggression from the North.

*Relations Between the Two Koreas*

The relationship between North and South Korea has featured hostility and suspicion since the end of World War II. South Koreans remember that in 1950 Kim Il-sung called for a "peaceful dialogue" to reunite the peninsula only days before North Korean tanks rolled across the border and devastated the South. Ever since, both sides have aspired to reunification, each tendering proposals, but they have been reluctant to make any concession that might endanger their safety.[26]

In the early 1970s, the United States made overtures to the PRC, withdrew the 7th Division from the peninsula, and gave signs of retreating from its commitment to defend East Asian nations. This persuaded the leadership of the ROK to undertake its own defense. Seoul thus undertook initiatives that would permit representatives from both Koreas to discuss ways of peacefully reuniting the peninsula.

The North Koreans had concerns of their own that contributed to their disposition to enter into dialogue with the South. The Soviet Union and the PRC were involved in a protracted and acrimonious conflict that included firefights along the Sino-Soviet border. Pyongyang could no longer count on its "proletarian" allies for support in the event of hostilities.

Whatever motives inspired them, the dialogue during the early 1970s was full of mutual recriminations. Worse still, engaging in dialogue did not inhibit the DPRK's efforts to undermine the ROK government through organized subversion, support of insurrectionists and saboteurs, and preparations for invasion. DPRK infiltration tunnels, for example, were dug during the period of "peaceful dialogue," clashes at sea between DPRK naval vessels and ROK fishing boats occurred, and a DPRK spy vessel was sunk off Pusan in December 1973.

A new effort was made in the early 1980s to pursue dialogue in the service of "peaceful reunification," but with equally poor results. During that period, DPRK officials hired two Canadian mercenaries to assassinate President Chun (the attempt failed), and in October 1983, three DPRK army officers attempted to assassinate Chun on his state visit to Burma, killing seventeen members of the presidential party. To add insult to criminal outrage, Pyongyang celebrated the activities of the Revolutionary Party for Reunification, a radical South Korean organization subservient to the DPRK.

Moreover, throughout this period, ROK security forces regularly intercepted DPRK agents attempting to infiltrate the South. In 1980, for example, counter-espionage agents in Japan arrested members of a conspiracy to infiltrate DPRK spies and terrorists into the ROK.

The unfortunate conclusion is that efforts at dialogue do not reduce the threat that shadows the ROK. The measure of the threat can be estimated by the instances of overt hostility from the North, by the activities of DPRK agents in the South, and by the aggressive deployment of DPRK troops and weapons along the DMZ.

During a recent period of dialogue on reunification, the DPRK deployed Soviet-supplied Z5U-23/4 anti-aircraft weapons and SA-5 anti-aircraft missiles, which have an effective range of two hundred miles, within seventy miles of Seoul. Rapid-deployment and special-forces brigades are poised for incursion into the South. Over 40 percent of the DPRK's air assets are based in airfields minutes away from the DMZ, and 70 percent of its naval forces are in forward-staging areas. The recent provision of the advanced MiG-29s by the Soviet Union adds significantly to the North's capabilities, and new helicopter landing pads along the DMZ further threaten the defense forces of the South. As a consequence, a Washington analyst maintained that the military threat facing the ROK in 1988 was "greater . . . than at any time since the Carter administration threatened to withdraw U.S. troops" in 1977.[27]

The authorities in Seoul have good reason to be concerned. The DPRK has made very clear that it intends to "do away with the colonial fascist rule of the U.S. imperialists and their stooges in South Korea."[28] When explicit intentions are joined with evident capabilities, responsible leadership must take measures to offset the risks.

The authorities in Seoul have nevertheless persisted in their negotiations with the DPRK. Ongoing discussions could conceivably influence the political leaders in the North; continued contact might reduce the risk of aggression. Moreover, both Chun Doo-hwan and Roh Tae-woo have prevailed on the United States to reaffirm its commitment to maintain the 2nd Division along the DMZ as a deterrent. Finally, South Korea has continued with its force modernization program, so that in the reasonably near future, the armed forces of the ROK will themselves constitute a credible deterrent to North Korean attack.

Other than the continued arms buildup in the North, and its apparent support by the Soviet Union, the most troubling development influencing relations between the two Koreas has been the mounting opposition by radical students in the ROK to the presence of U.S. troops and the students' support of the DPRK's approach to reunification. The students' anti-Americanism is couched in the familiar vocabulary of Marxism-Leninism. The United States is the culprit that divided the peninsula after World War II, after which it exploited the dependency of the ROK to profit economically and to use its "puppets" in Seoul to support its "paranoid anti-communism."[29] The cries are "Yankee go home!" and "Down with the military fascists!"

The radical students by themselves would have little effect on their nation had not recent developments made some segments of the population susceptible to student influence.

Trade friction between the United States and the Republic of Korea has certainly had a negative effect. In the ROK, farmers are incensed by Washington's insistence that the Korean market be opened to U.S. farm produce, and manufacturers, many of whom are confined by size or non-competitiveness to the domestic market, object to U.S. attempts to introduce more U.S. exports into the republic.

Further exacerbating the tensions is Washington's insistence that the ROK pay more of the cost of stationing U.S. troops on its soil. Seoul maintains that this would only fuel anti-U.S. sentiments, given the heavy taxes already paid by ROK citizens.[30]

In fact, surveys show a decline in pro-U.S. sentiment and an increase in anti-U.S. feeling in the ROK. By mid-1988, 16 percent of respondents in a probability sample of South Koreans indicated that they disliked the United States—up from 3 percent in 1984, and only 37 percent indicated that they were pro-American—down from 70 percent a scant four years ago.[31]

Such feelings have become so widespread that some of the major political figures in the ROK have taken up the cause. Kim Dae-jung, for example, has deplored U.S. "interference" in Korean politics and has urged drastic changes in U.S. policy.[32]

In the increasingly open political environment, radical students have been able to channel vague anti-American sentiments into the service of DPRK policy, thereby increasing the threat faced by the South. More dangerous, perhaps, is the readiness of student agitators to act in ways that could precipitate crisis. Radical students, for example, have attempted to cross the DMZ and undertake a "people's reunification" of the peninsula. This could easily create an incendiary situation involving all the armed forces deployed along the border.

In ROK cities, radical students have become so hysterical that some of them have self-immolated in service of the "cause." Each such tragedy dims the prospects of rational deliberation, compromise, and political planning.

The problems are compounded by some Korean and foreign clerics who have further inflamed passions. These "progressive" churchmen have charged ROK's political leaders with "breaking the will and spirit" of the people in order to satisfy the needs of "people on Wall Street and in the Pentagon." Animated by a seemingly irrepressible "anti-anti-communism," the representatives of "people's theology" have advocated a withdrawal of U.S. troops from the peninsula because their presence does not serve the "interests of the Korean people."[33]

Thus, at a critical juncture in the history of the republic, when the community faces difficult political adjustments, tries to address serious social problems, and attempts to effect structural changes in its economy, the leadership is forced to meet not only an external military threat but also a domestic threat— dissidents dedicated to subversive actions. All the accomplishments of the evolving system have been placed in jeopardy. At a time when the realization of political democracy is within grasp, the future of the republic has been put at risk.

The authorities in Seoul face a dilemma. If they attempt to suppress domestic dissidence, they will face negative international reaction and the possibility that their efforts could escalate the violence beyond control. Defusing the domestic threat will require a rapid resolution of prevailing difficulties, satisfying the demands of the majority and isolating subversives while allowing them their full democratic rights. None of that will be easy.

The political authorities in Seoul will have to demonstrate a tolerance and patience unusual in the best of circumstances. Effective policy can only come from non-partisan agreement among all the major political figures in the republic. To that end, the leadership has undertaken briefing sessions with all major political parties to inform them on the most urgent economic, social, and security problems that face the nation.

This action is intended to produce not only a coherent policy dealing with general problems but a specific response to the irresponsible conduct of radical students and their mentors. The hope is that a consensus policy will keep politicians from exploiting the opportunities created by the inflammatory behavior of the radicals.

The ROK is close to attaining the goals that have inspired almost every less-developed nation in the world. At its current pace, it will soon be among the world's top ten trading nations. There is every reason to believe that it will also enjoy all the benefits of political democracy.

The attainment of those goals is threatened by the factors briefly considered above, but the greatest threat lies in DPRK aggression. The DPRK will soon face great domestic tension with the death of Kim Il-sung, the "sagacious Dear Comrade Leader to whom all Koreans must remain loyal generation after generation for eternity."[34] At the same time, the ROK's force modernization program is gradually eliminating the DPRK's military option.

If political instability and radical posturing in the South were to be interpreted by the DPRK as a lack of resolve, the result might well be fateful. The DPRK invasion in 1950 was the result of a similar set of circumstances. To achieve complete control at home, Kim Il-sung required a cause around which all factions could be mobilized. The United States had communicated its general indifference to the fate of the ROK by withdrawing its troops from the peninsula, and political unrest in the republic suggested that there would be no unity in defense. The attack followed.

The consequences of a successful war on the ROK are clear. The testimony of Kampuchea, Laos, and Vietnam is too recent to leave doubts about the fate of Koreans under the ministrations of a victorious Kim Il-sung or his heirs. For the United States, the results would be almost as disastrous—an economic, political, security, and moral tragedy for all Americans.

# 6
# *Implications for U.S. Policy*

UNITED STATES POLICY towards Korea must be formulated with a clear recognition that important economic and security interests are at stake. On the economic side, a protectionist policy that reduces South Korean access to U.S. markets can only be counter-productive. The appearance of vindictiveness that attends U.S. protectionism, moreover, feeds the latent anti-Americanism that threatens to become an important factor in South Korean politics. When Choi Chang-yoon, vice minister of culture and information, reflected on the growth of anti-Americanism in the Republic of Korea in 1988, he laid the blame on trade tensions, and their exploitation by those intent upon exacerbating U.S.-ROK difficulties.

*Economic Issues*

According to Rha Woong-bae, minister of trade and industry, rapid trade liberalization, particularly with respect to agricultural products, could "have adverse political consequences"; the government in Seoul would therefore have to move "cautiously."[1] Among ROK families, 25 percent depend on farm income for their standard of living. An increase in farm imports could dramatically increase anti-American sentiments and destabilize support of the government.

The ROK government has recently made substantial good faith gestures in trade liberalization. As far back as 1986, there was a 50 percent reduction in the average tariff rate on incoming goods. Efforts have also been made to increase purchases from U.S. suppliers to reduce the trade imbalance. In February 1988, new policy directives on trade and current accounts strove to promote more equitable trade relations with major trading partners, particularly the United States. A trade mission to the United States was organized in mid-1988, with plans to purchase $2.6 billion of U.S. goods and services. The purchases were to include over $700 million in wheat, corn, soybean, and raw cotton, about $700 million in imports of U.S. electronic testing equipment and producer goods, and a further $450 million in U.S. equipment for SMI firms.

By mid-1988, the Republic of Korea was supplementing its "buy American" purchasing missions with a trade policy that required government agencies and public institutions to purchase U.S. products rather than any alternatives. South Korea also pledged to purchase more U.S. agricultural commodities; the United States now supplies the ROK with more than 60 percent of its agricultural imports. Finally, the government encouraged the private sector to increase its imports of machinery, raw materials, and spare parts from the United States. As an incentive, the government has offered new foreign-currency loans to support these imports. These policies, together with wide-ranging tariff reductions, increased protection for U.S. intellectual property, the opening of the ROK market to U.S. service industries, the reduction of export financing, and voluntary export constraint, have eased trade friction. In fact, a major review of trade relations undertaken by the United States in mid-1989 did not identify South Korea as a flagrant violator nor did it recommend sanctions against the ROK.

Unfortunately for South Korea, ROK products have recently stopped receiving the advantages of the Generalized System of Preferences (GSP) that allowed them to enter the U.S. market largely without tariff restrictions. In January 1989, the Republic of Korea was "graduated" out of the class of developing nations.

Protectionist sentiment and legitimate grievance have combined to mobilize sufficient public support in the United States to reduce the ROK's access to the American market. While the ROK conglomerates will be competitive enough to penetrate that market, the SMIs may have considerable difficulties. Their failure may have very serious political repercussions in the

ROK, fueling anti-Americanism and instability. However, an expansion of South Korea's domestic market might help offset the discontinuance of tariff-free entry into the United States. And a rise in the average wage of industrial workers in the ROK would contribute to the nation's stability and economic viability. Whatever the case, the United States should be aware of the implications of its trade policies. The decision to "graduate" the republic out of the GSP was taken unilaterally, without consultation with Seoul, an insensitive action on Washington's part.

Trade issues will be central to U.S.-ROK relations for the immediate future. Dealing with them effectively will require all the diplomatic skills and goodwill of the executive branch and the foreign service agencies of the United States. Prevailing U.S. deficits and trade imbalances have made trade with the ROK a major political issue. But trade issues cannot be addressed without recognizing that they impact on other issues no less vital to both countries and of critical importance to the future of the entire region.

One example can be found in Washington's treatment of ROK arms sales on the international market. Because the ROK's arms industries produce weapon systems and munitions involving U.S. designs or components, the United States controls the trade. In the past, for a variety of reasons, the United States has been reluctant to allow the ROK to market its products. In 1981–1982, Seoul requested permission to market about $55 million in arms; Washington approved less than $2 million in sales.[2]

It is difficult to justify such restrictions. The DPRK is a major arms supplier to the less-developed countries. It sustains its substantial arms industries with foreign exchange earned by sales on the international arms market. Longer production runs of weapon systems reduce per unit cost and make the entire enterprise more economically viable.

For years Pyongyang has supported its own military by foreign arms sales; for example, about $800 million in DPRK arms have been shipped to Iran and $400 million to Zimbabwe.[3] As a result, DPRK war industries have flourished while those in the

ROK increasingly have become "nonperforming assets"—an economically burdensome necessity.

Unlike Japan, which allocates about 1 percent of its GNP to defense, the Republic of Korea spends 5 or 6 percent. The ROK no longer receives low-interest military sales credits from the United States, but must purchase arms at full cost. Moreover, unlike Japan, the ROK has a substantial foreign debt whose servicing consumes about 20 percent of its foreign exchange earnings. While the economy of the ROK is basically sound, the ROK is not Japan, and arguments that can be mounted against Japan concerning trade surpluses cannot be used against the ROK.

The Republic of Korea must carefully monitor its economy, and its foreign exchange earnings are critical to successful performance. Arms transfers could be an important component of foreign sales.

The United States provides the largest single market for ROK goods and influences its trading opportunities in a variety of ways. The Republic of Korea is the seventh largest trading partner of the United States and its future is inextricably tied to U.S. policy decisions. The failure of that policy could generate political tensions that might jeopardize the future of both countries.

Some economists and policy analysts have suggested that the United States might enter into a free-trade association with the ROK to facilitate mutually beneficial trade and commercial activity. That relationship, which holds the prospect of a number of economic and political benefits, has been established with Israel and Canada. In fact, such an association involving the United States, the Republic of Korea, and Japan would unite the world's most successful economies in one dynamic combination.

*Regional Security*

Such a free-trade association would contribute to the general stabilization of the entire region. Although the emphasis would be on economic relations, the association would have obvious security implications as well. The United States and Japan would become deeply involved in the economic life of the ROK.

Neither the Soviet Union nor the PRC would be likely to underwrite DPRK military aggression on the peninsula under those conditions.

The PRC, in fact, has given evidence of an interest in stabilizing the Korean peninsula by embarking on broad-gauged informal relations with the ROK. Trade between the PRC and the ROK exceeded $1.3 billion in 1986 and will exceed $3 billion a year by the end of the 1980s.

While Beijing formally supports the DPRK's position on the reunification of the peninsula, Chinese communists give every indication of viewing the U.S. military presence as a stabilizing factor. The PRC leadership would not welcome a unified Korea dominated by a pro-Moscow regime, because the Korean peninsula has always provided an invasion corridor into Northeastern China. As long as the DPRK is dependent on Soviet aid, Pyongyang will be very susceptible to Moscow's influence. (North Korea now receives over 60 percent of its electricity, 50 percent of its oil, 40 percent of its steel products, and over 35 percent of its rolling products from the Soviet Union; and an estimated three thousand Soviet technicians are assisting DPRK heavy industry, having supervised the construction and maintenance of sixty-two major factories, including power stations and oil processing facilities in Pyongyang, Pukchang, and Unggi.[4])

Given these circumstances, it would seem a propitious time to undertake initiatives that might stabilize the military situation on the peninsula. A non-aggression agreement between the two Koreas has much to recommend it. Irrespective of the reunification negotiations, an agreement by both sides to abjure violence could only enhance the prospects of peace. Cross-recognition, in which both political communities on the peninsula would be accorded diplomatic recognition by the major nations in the region, could also reduce the likelihood of conflict. The admission of both Korean states into the United Nations is a third possibility that should be pursued.

The DPRK, unfortunately, has regularly objected to most of these suggestions, preferring to move swiftly to a "confederation" that would combine the two states, the two societies, and the two economies in some sort of political unity. Such a confederation would provide the disciplined North with a number of advantages that would threaten the politically undisciplined South with subordination to the North. The ROK, generally supported by the United States, has always recommended a gradual approach to reunification—suggesting family visits, economic exchanges, and a free flow of information as initial points of departure.

At the present time the situation is in considerable flux. While Washington has been loathe to negotiate with the DPRK directly, the possibility of contact between American and DPRK diplomats under carefully controlled circumstances opened up as early as 1987. Some indirect trade relations have already been established between the United States and the DPRK. It is evident that a great deal will depend on the Soviet Union, and Moscow's position is unclear.

The most fundamental interests of the United States, Japan, and the PRC are served by peace and stability on the Korean peninsula. Only the Soviet Union would gain considerable security advantage should the DPRK dominate the entire peninsula.

Moscow has little incentive to precipitate major changes through conflict in Korea at this time. The risks involved would be very high given the sensitivity and complexity of the relations between the major powers. Moscow may even deem it necessary to discourage Pyongyang from any further acts of violence against the South, to ensure the stability of the entire region.

The Soviet Union has dramatically improved its situation in East Asia since the early 1970s. It deploys a military capability on its northeastern coast and in peninsular Southeast Asia; it has reached an accommodation with the PRC; its relations with Vietnam are good; it has established security and economic ties with Laos, Kampuchea, India, and Afghanistan; and it has enhanced its connections with the Aquino administration in Manila. This favorable trend argues against any military adventure in the region.

The United States, in turn, has some reason for qualified optimism. The economic successes of Japan, the ROK, and the Republic of China on Taiwan all contribute to the prospects of democracy. Command economies and communist systems seem to have failed. The Soviets and the communist Chinese have had to introduce some elements of capitalism to salvage their economies.

The non-communist economies of the Association of South East Asian Nations (ASEAN), on the other hand, show every promise of attaining the same levels of growth and industrialization as those of the "miraculous" performers—South Korea and Taiwan. In almost every case, the prospect of democracy attends the economic success. And the combination of spectacular economic performance with increasing democratization has attracted other developing nations to the advantages of market-governed economic modalities and political democracy.

Unfortunately, a political crisis in the ROK or a military provocation by the DPRK could irrevocably alter the future prospects of the entire region. To offset these possibilities, the United States must provide every assistance to the ROK economy. Political stability, in large part, will depend on economic success.

To reduce the military threat from the North, the United States must maintain a military presence in the ROK. While air and naval forces, as well as command, control, communication, and intelligence capabilities, constitute the most important components of that presence, U.S. troops also provide a major disincentive to DPRK aggression.[5]

The U.S. role in the command structure of the forces, however, could be modified. At the present time an American general commands the combined U.S. and ROK forces, although 90 percent of the personnel are Korean. Coupled with the high visibility of the U.S. military command headquarters in central Seoul, the image is one of U.S. dominance.

Some adjustments could be made. The commander of combined forces should probably be an American, given the U.S. responsibilities, but more Korean officers could be assigned senior command positions. (Early in 1989, a decision was made to move U.S. military headquarters to a less visible locale.)

The United States should not underestimate the importance of the anti-Americanism of student radicalism and its destabilizing potential. To defuse the spread of anti-Americanism, the

United States must avoid the appearance of attempting to impose its will on Seoul, both economically and in terms of security. Washington must regularly consult with the ROK leadership and act only after bilateral negotiation and deliberation. In the past, this has not always been the case.

*Conclusions*

The prosperity of the Republic of Korea exemplifies the success of market-governed economies. The *Economist* of London has identified the ROK as one of the ten best countries in the world in which to live.[6] The republic is one of the major trading partners of the United States, and American venture capitalists and entrepreneurs have substantial investments in it. Finally, the Republic of Korea is critical to the strategic stability of East Asia; much depends on its continued survival and prosperity.

Credible deterrence is necessary to maintain stability in East Asia. The Democratic People's Republic of Korea has continually flouted international norms of behavior. Its aggression against the South—terrorist strikes, assassination attempts, forward-deployed special forces—are real and urgent threats. The presence of U.S. forces on the ground along the DMZ gives warning of Washington's resolve and deters full-blown attack.

Ever since the Nixon-Sato communique of 1969, Japan has made clear its concern with the security of the ROK. Hostile forces in the ROK would threaten the Japanese home islands of Kyushu and Honshu; friendly forces protect the sea-lanes on which Japan's economy depends. Like the Republic of China on Taiwan, the ROK is essential to the long-term security of Japan.

Deterrence in East Asia depends, in large part, on the security relationship between the United States, Japan, and the ROK. In a relationship troubled by a colonial past, South Koreans and Japanese will have to pursue more effective security cooperation in terms of joint operations, combined exercises, command and control functions, and early warning capabilities.

Although the Soviet Union is experimenting with internal and foreign policy reform, the United States and its allies must maintain a military capability in East Asia sufficient to make aggression too costly to consider. The recent apparently conciliatory moves made by the Soviet Union in Afghanistan and Vietnam seem to recognize the high risks involved in armed confrontation.

The United States has long shouldered the chief burden of holding back the spread of Marxist-Leninist systems. In East Asia its sure allies have been Japan, the Republic of China on Taiwan, and the Republic of Korea. The future will require that those nations increase their contributions to the joint enterprise. The ROK stands out among those nations.

In the struggle to resist the expansion of totalitarianism, the ROK has contributed much in blood and treasure. For almost half a century, Koreans sacrificed life and property in the struggle against Japanese imperialism. For almost as long, South Koreans have resisted the aggressions of communism. Moreover, by dint of impressive collective effort and considerable sacrifice, the ROK people have sown the seeds of democracy and prosperity. This generation may not see the New Korea, but the sacrifice of five generations testifies to its ultimate realization. That Americans will have contributed to it should be a matter of no small satisfaction.[7] Thousands of young Americans fell alongside hundreds of thousands of Koreans in defense of the same vision—a New Korea. The obligation of the present generation of Americans and Koreans is to pursue a policy that will not betray that sacrifice and that vision.

# Notes

### Chapter One

1. For general histories of Korea, see Frederick A. McKenzie, *The Tragedy of Korea* (Seoul: Yonsei University, 1975); Han Woo-keun, *The History of Korea* (Honolulu: University Press of Hawaii, 1971); and William E. Henthorn, *A History of Korea* (New York: Free Press, 1971).

2. For a review of the early relations of Korea with its neighbors, see Chun Hae-jong, "A Historical Survey of the Sino-Korean Tributary Relationship," *Journal of Social Sciences and Humanities* 25 (December 1966), pp. 1–31; and Frederick M. Nelson, *Korea and the Old Order in Eastern Asia* (Baton Rouge: Louisiana State University Press, 1945).

3. For the U.S. evaluation of Korea's strategic position, see General A. G. Wedemeyer, *Korea: Report to the President* (Washington: Government Printing Office, 1951); and *Military Situation in the Far East* (Washington: Joint Senate Committee on Armed Service and Foreign Relations, 82nd Congress, 1st Session), pp. 1988–1990.

4. *Selected Works of Mao Tsetung* (Beijing: Foreign Languages, 1977), pp. 5, 39.

5. This summary account is taken from A. T. Mahan, *The Problem of Asia and Its Effects upon International Policies* (London: Sampson Low, Martston and Company, 1900).

6. See the discussion in William E. Livezey, *Mahan on Sea Power* (Norman: University of Oklahoma Press, 1981), pp. 206–223. George Kennan's rationale for containment is found in "The Sources of Soviet Conflict," *Foreign Affairs,* July 1947.

7. A. James Gregor and Maria Hsia Chang, *The Iron Triangle: A U.S. Security Policy for Northeast Asia* (Stanford: Hoover Institution Press, 1984), pp. 58–59.

8. For a detailed treatment of the Independence Society, see the doctoral dissertation of Vipan Chandra, "Nationalism and Popular Participation in Government in Late 19th-Century Korea: The Contribution of the Independence Club (1896–98)" (Harvard University, 1977); and Chandra's article, "The Independence Club and Korea's First Proposal for a National Legislative Assembly," *Occasional Papers on Korea* 4 (September 1975), pp. 19–35.

9. For a more extensive discussion, see Eugene C. I. Kim and Han-kyo

Kim, *Korea and the Politics of Imperialism, 1876–1910* (Berkeley: University of California Press, 1975); and George A. McGrane, *Korea's Tragic Hours: The Closing Years of the Yi Dynasty* (Seoul: Taewon, 1973).

10. Baik Bong, *Kim Il Sung: Biography* (Tokyo: Miraisha, 1970), vol. 3, p. 641, and vol. 1, ch. 2.

11. Ibid., vol. 3, pp. 156, 157.

12. See John H. Kautsky, *Communism and the Politics of Development: Persistent Myths and Changing Behavior* (New York: John Wiley, 1968).

13. See Irving Louis Horowitz, *Three Worlds of Development: The Theory and Practice of International Stratification* (New York: Oxford University Press, 1966), p. 126.

14. Paul A. Baran, *The Political Economy of Growth* (New York: Monthly Review Press, 1957), p. 261.

15. Gunnar Myrdal, *Development and Underdevelopment* (Cairo: Cairo University Press, 1956), p. 63.

16. W. W. Rostow, *The Stages of Economic Growth: A Non-Communist Manifesto* (New York: Cambridge University Press, 1969), pp. 30, 24–25. The volume consists of lectures given in the late 1950s.

17. Y. S. Brenner, *Theories of Economic Development and Growth* (London: George Allen and Unwin, 1969), ch. 4.

18. Ichiro Nakayama, *Industrialization of Japan* (Honolulu: East-West Center, 1963).

19. Joungwon Kim, *Divided Korea: The Politics of Development, 1945–1972* (Cambridge: Harvard University Press, 1975), p. 171.

20. Thomas H. Kang, "Changes in the North Korean Personality from Confucian to Communist," in Jae Kyu Park and Jung Gun Kim, eds., *The Politics of North Korea* (Seoul: Kyungnam University, 1979), pp. 77–80.

21. See John Merrill, "Internal Warfare in Korea," in Bruce Cumings, ed., *Child of Conflict: The Korean American Relationship, 1943–1953* (Seattle: University of Washington Press, 1983), pp. 133–162.

22. Baik Bong, *Kim Il Sung*, vol. 3, ch. 1.

23. "Introduction," in Edward S. Mason et al., *The Economic and Social Modernization of the Republic of Korea* (Cambridge: Harvard University Press, 1980), pp. 14–15.

24. Hakan Hedberg, *The New Challenge: South Korea!* (Seoul: Chongno Book Center, 1978), pp. 36–37.

## Chapter Two

1. Baik Bong, *Kim Il Sung: Biography* (Tokyo: Miraisha, 1970), vol. 3, pp. 29, 31, 625–626, 448–449.

2. Edward S. Mason et al., *The Economic and Social Modernization of the Republic of Korea* (Cambridge: Harvard University Press, 1980), p. 204.

3. Ralph N. Clough, *Embattled Korea: The Rivalry for International Support* (Boulder: Westview, 1987), p. 84.

4. As quoted in Baik Bong, *Kim Il Sung*, vol. 3, p. 32.

5. A. James Gregor, *The China Connection: U.S. Policy and the People's Republic of China* (Stanford: Hoover Institution Press, 1986), ch. 7.

6. Joungwon Kim, "The Peak of Socialism in North Korea: The Five and Seven Year Plans," *Asian Survey* 25, 5 (May 1985), pp. 262–263.
7. See Daniel S. Juhn, "A Survey of Economic Development of North Korea," in Jae Kyu Park and Jung Gun Kim, eds., *The Politics of North Korea* (Seoul: Kyungnam University, 1979), pp. 253–257.
8. See Mason, *Economic and Social Modernization*, pp. 237–243.
9. See *Joint Commission on Rural Reconstruction Report No. 1* (Taipei: JCCR, 1950), pp. 62–66.
10. John D. Montgomery, "United States Advocacy of International Land Reform," in Montgomery, ed., *International Dimensions of Land Reform* (Boulder: Westview, 1984), pp. 116–118.
11. See Clough, *Embattled Korea*, pp. 70–72.
12. All the quotations are from *Major Speeches by Korea's Park Chung Hee*, ed. Shin Bum Shik (Seoul: Hollym Corporation, 1970), pp. 121, 122, 142.
13. Ibid., pp. 21, 143.
14. Ibid., p. 208.
15. Sung Hwan Ban, Pal Yong Moon, and Dwight H. Perkins, *Rural Development: Studies in the Modernization of the Republic of Korea, 1945–1975* (Cambridge: Harvard University Press, 1980), p. 75.
16. Clough, *Embattled Korea*, p. 71.
17. Hakan Hedberg, *The New Challenge: South Korea!* (Seoul: Chongno Book Center, 1978), pp. 38–39.
18. Mason, *Economic and Social Modernization*, p. 254.
19. See Leroy P. Jones and Il SaKong, *Government, Business, and Entrepreneurship in Economic Development: The Korean Case* (Cambridge: Harvard University Press, 1980).
20. *Economic Statistics Yearbook, 1960–1976* (Seoul: Bank of Korea, 1977).
21. Mason, *Economic and Social Modernization*, p. 481.
22. *National Income in Korea, 1975* (Seoul: Bank of Korea, 1976), pp. 144–145.
23. See "In Defense of Freedom," in *Major Speeches*, pp. 34–40; see also pp. 256–260, 285–290.
24. Claude A. Buss, *The United States and the Republic of Korea: Background for Policy* (Stanford: Hoover Institution Press, 1982), p. 52.
25. See Dilip Mukerjee, *Lessons from Korea's Industrial Experience* (Kuala Lumpur: Institute of Strategic and International Studies, 1986), chs. 5 and 6.

## Chapter Three

1. Lucien Pye, *Aspects of Political Development* (Boston: Little, Brown, 1966), pp. 45–48.
2. For a more ample discussion, see A. James Gregor, *A Survey of Marxism* (New York: Random House, 1965), pp. 185–201.
3. Baik Bong, *Kim Il Sung: Biography* (Tokyo: Miraisha, 1970), vol. 3, pp. 636, 637, 638.
4. Ibid., vol. 1, p. 77, and vol. 3, p. 641.
5. Ibid., vol. 3, p. 667, n. 1; "Constitution of the Democratic People's

Republic of Korea," Articles 2 and 4, in Jae Kuy Park and Jung Gun Kim, *The Politics of North Korea* (Seoul: Kyungman University, 1979), p. 639.

6. Baik Bong, *Kim Il Sung,* vol. 3, p. 639; and "Constitution," Articles 50–54, 10, 67, 71.

7. Kim Il-sung, as quoted in Park and Kim, *Politics of North Korea,* p. 126.

8. See Baik Bong, *Kim Il Sung,* vol. 3, ch. 3.3.

9. Park and Kim, *Politics of North Korea,* p. 132.

10. Baik Bong, *Kim Il Sung,* vol. 3, pp. 261–267.

11. Ibid., pp. 273, 274, 276.

12. See the annual reports of Amnesty International and those of Raymond D. Gastil, ed., *Freedom in the World: Political Rights and Civil Liberties.*

13. See Jeffrey W. Barrett, *Impulse to Revolution in Latin America* (New York: Praeger, 1985), p. 235.

14. An early statement of this position is found in P. T. Bauer, *Dissent on Development* (Cambridge: Harvard University Press, 1976). A more recent discussion can be found in Jan S. Prybyla, *Market and Plan Under Socialism* (Stanford: Hoover Institution Press, 1987).

15. Choi Sok-wu, "Reception of *Sohak* (Western Learning) in Korea," in Chun Shin-yong, ed., *Korean Thought* (Seoul: Si-sa-yong-o-sa, 1982), pp. 81–94; and Lee Wu-song, "The Rise of *Silhak Thought,*" in ibid., pp. 55–64.

16. For a discussion of Liang's views, see Philip C. Huang, *Liang Ch'i-ch'ao and Modern Chinese Liberalism* (Seattle: University of Washington Press, 1972), chs. 2, 4, 6, 7. For a discussion of Sun's program of economic growth and industrialization, see A. James Gregor and Maria Hsia Chang, *Ideology and Development: Sun Yat-sen and the Economic History of Taiwan* (Berkeley: University of California Press, 1980).

17. Choi Sok-wu, "Reception of *Sohak,*" p. 84.

18. For a short biography of So, see Channing Liem, *America's Finest Gift to Korea: The Life of Philip Jaisohn* (New York: William-Frederick, 1952).

19. Young Il Shin, "American Protestant Missions to Korea and the Awakening of Political and Social Consciousness in the Koreans Between 1884 and 1941," in Kwak Tae-hwan, ed., *U.S.-Korean Relations, 1882–1982* (Seoul: Kyungnam University, 1982), pp. 196–219.

20. A collection of Rhee's public pronouncements after assuming the presidency of the ROK can be found in *Flaming High: Excerpts from Statements by President Syngman Rhee, 1953–1955* (Seoul: Office of Public Information, 1956), 2 vols. For an account of Rhee's life, see Robert T. Oliver, *Syngman Rhee: The Man Behind the Myth* (New York: Dodd, Mead, 1954).

21. See Han Shik Park, "Two Ideologies in One Culture: The Prospect for National Integration in Korea," in Tai-Hean Kwak, Chonghan Kim, and Hong Nack Kim, eds., *Korean Reunification: New Perspectives and Approaches* (Seoul: Kyungnam University, 1984), pp. 123–149.

22. Dilip Mukerjee, *Lessons from Korea's Industrial Experience* (Kuala Lumpur: Institute of Strategic and International Studies, 1986), p. 13.

23. Charles E. Lindbloom, "Economics and the Administration of National Planning," *Public Administration Review* 23 (December 1965), pp. 244–283.

24. See In-jung Whang, "Elites and Economic Programs: A Study of Changing Leadership for Economic Development in Korea, 1955–1967" (Ph.D.

thesis, University of Pittsburgh, 1967); Yoon-tai Kim, "A Study of Korean Higher Civil Servants and Some Proposals for Reforming the Bureaucratic System," *Korean Journal of Public Administration* 4 (1966), pp. 243–265; and L. I. Wade and Bong Sik Kim, *The Political Economy of Success: Public Policy Development in the Republic of Korea* (Seoul: Kyung Hee University, 1977), chs. 4, 5.

25. Ramgopal Agarwala, *Planning in Developing Countries* (Washington: World Bank, 1983), pp. 13, 17.

26. See John G. Stoessinger, *Crusaders and Pragmatists: Movers of Modern American Foreign Policy* (New York: Norton, 1979), ch. 8.

27. See A. James Gregor and Maria Hsia Chang, *The Republic of China and U.S. Policy* (Washington: Ethics and Public Policy Center, 1983); and John F. Copper, *A Quiet Revolution: Political Development in the Republic of China* (Washington: Ethics and Public Policy Center, 1988).

28. See A. James Gregor, *In the Shadow of Giants: The Nations of Southeast Asia and the Major Powers* (Stanford: Hoover Institution Press, in press).

## Chapter Four

1. V. I. Lenin, as quoted in Arthur Schlesinger, Jr., "Origins of the Cold War," in Vernon V. Aspaturian, ed., *Process and Power in Soviet Foreign Policy* (Boston: Little, Brown, 1971), pp. 233–234; and J. V. Stalin, "Berlin Crisis, the U.N. and Anglo-American Aggressive Policies, and Churchill," *Pravda,* 28 October 1948, and "When Is War Not Inevitable?" *Pravda,* 16 February 1951, in *For Peaceful Coexistence: Postwar Interviews* (New York: International, 1951), pp. 38–39.

2. Mao Zedong, "Revolutionary Forces of the World Unite, Fight Against Imperialist Aggression," in *Selected Works* (Beijing: Foreign Language, 1967), vol. 4, pp. 284–285; and "Cast Away Illusions, Prepare for Struggle," in ibid., pp. 428, 429–430.

3. Liu Shaoqi, *Internationalism and Nationalism* (Beijing: Foreign Languages, 1951), p. 21.

4. Ibid., pp. 4, 15–16, 19.

5. Ibid., p. 34.

6. See Young Whan Kihl, *Politics and Policies in Divided Korea: Regimes in Contest* (Boulder: Westview, 1984), p. 31.

7. See A. James Gregor, "Soviet Capabilities in East Asia," in *Security of the Sea Lanes of Asia* (Washington: International Security Council, 1986), pp. 17–30.

8. Shinn Rinn-sup, *Area Handbook for North Korea* (Washington: Government Printing Office, 1969), p. 298.

9. As quoted in Yung-hwa Jo and Ralph Marshall, "Linkage Sources of North Korean Foreign Policy," in Jae Kyu Park and Jung Gun Kim, eds., *The Politics of North Korea* (Seoul: Kyungnam University, 1979), pp. 169–170.

10. See Kihl, *Politics and Policies,* p. 147.

11. Ralph N. Clough, *Embattled Korea: The Rivalry for International Support* (Boulder: Westview, 1987), p. 105.

12. *World Military Expenditures and Arms Transfers, 1971–1980* (Washington: U.S. Arms Control and Disarmament Agency, 1983), p. 55.
13. Richard Nixon, *U.S. Foreign Policy for the 1970s: A New Strategy for Peace* (Washington: Government Printing Office, 1970), pp. 55–56.
14. Gregory F. T. Winn, "Riding the Tiger: Military Confrontation on the Korean Peninsula," in Tae-hwan Kwak et al., eds., *U.S.-Korean Relations, 1882–1982* (Seoul: Kyungnam University, 1982), pp. 268–270. See also Tae-hwan Kwak, "U.S.-Korean Security Relations," in ibid., pp. 223–236.
15. See A. James Gregor and Maria H. Chang, *The Iron Triangle: A U.S. Security Policy for Northeast Asia* (Stanford: Hoover Institution Press, 1984), ch. 5.
16. See Norman Polmar, "The Navy of Democratic People's Republic of Korea," in Barry M. Blechman and Robert P. Berman, eds., *Guide to Far Eastern Navies* (Annapolis: Naval Institute Press, 1978), pp. 314–333.
17. Kihl, *Politics and Policies*, p. 177.
18. Baik Bong, *Kim Il Sung: Biography* (Tokyo: Miraisha, 1970), vol. 3, pp. 642, 643, 640.
19. Larry A. Niksch, "The Military Balance on the Korean Peninsula," in *Korea and World Affairs* (Boulder: Westview, 1988), pp. 270–271.
20. See Mark L. Urban, "The North Korean People's Army: Anatomy of a Giant," *International Defense Review*, July 1983, pp. 927–932.
21. See the summary account in John M. Collins, *U.S.-Soviet Military Balance, 1980–1985* (New York: Pergamon-Brassey, 1985), pp. 3–6.
22. See Viktor Suvorov, *Inside the Soviet Army* (London: Grafton, 1982), pp. 218–225.
23. Joseph Churba, *Soviet Breakout: Strategies to Meet It* (New York: Pergamon-Brassey, 1988), ch. 8, and *Security Policy in East Asia: A Politico-Military Assessment, 1988* (New York: International Security Council, 1988).
24. *Speech by Mikhail Gorbachev in Vladivostok, July 28, 1986* (Moscow: Novosti, 1986), pp. 34–35, 18, 20, 27.
25. See Hyung-hwa Lyon, *Peace and Unification in Korea and International Law* (Baltimore: University of Maryland School of Law, 1986), pp. 105–111; and Kim Il-sung, *For the Independent Peaceful Reunification of Korea* (New York: International, 1975), pp. 211–216. See also *A White Paper on South-North Dialogue in Korea* (Seoul: National Unification Board, 1982).
26. Masao Horie and Katsuichi Tsukamoto, "Japan, Korea, and U.S. Relations in the Far East Region," in *Strategic Implications of the Soviet-North Korean Alliance* (New York: International Security Council, 1987), pp. 32–33.
27. Manabu Yoshida, "Changing Relations Between North Korea and the Soviet Navy," in *Strategic Implications*, pp. 83–87.
28. See A. James Gregor, *Arming the Dragon: U.S. Security Ties with the People's Republic of China* (Washington: Ethics and Public Policy Center, 1988), chs. 2, 3.
29. Kim Il-sung, *Report of the Sixth Congress of the Workers' Party of Korea on the Work of the Central Committee, October 10, 1980* (Pyongyang: Foreign Languages, 1980), pp. 59–81.
30. Donald S. Zagoria, "The Superpowers and Korea," in Ilpyong J. Kim, ed., *The Strategic Triangle: China, the United States, and the Soviet Union* (New York: Paragon, 1987), p. 176.

31. See Leonard Silk, "Pressures to Cut Military Spending," *New York Times,* 3 June 1988, p. D2; Arnold Beichman, "A Hard Look at Soviet Forces," *Washington Times,* 7 September 1988, p. F4; and Bill Gertz, "Soviet Defense Spending Belies Rhetoric," ibid., 13 September 1988, p. A3.

32. Zagoria, "The Superpowers and Korea," p. 176.

## Chapter Five

1. "North Korea," *Asia 1988 Yearbook* (Hong Kong: Far Eastern Economic Review, 1988), p. 161.

2. Young Whan Kihl, *Politics and Policies in Divided Korea: Regimes in Contest* (Boulder: Westview, 1984), table 6.5, p. 142.

3. See John Greenwald, "The Big Shakeup," *Time,* 8 August 1988, pp. 202–222.

4. See Choi Chang-yoon, "Political Development in Korea: Achievements and Prospects," in *The Heritage Lectures* (Washington: Heritage Foundation, 1987).

5. Hong Mack and Sunki Choe, "Urbanization and Changing Voting Patterns in South Korean Parliamentary Elections," in Ilpyong J. Kim and Young Whan Kihl, eds., *Political Change in South Korea* (Washington: Paragon House, 1988), table 1, p. 160.

6. Robert A. Kinney, "Students, Intellectuals, and the Churches: Their Roles in Korean Politics," *Asian Affairs* 8 (January-February 1981), p. 184.

7. "Will Success Spoil the South Korean Church?," *Christianity Today,* 20 November 1987, p. 32.

8. Wonmo Dong, "University Students in South Korean Politics: Patterns of Radicalization in the 1980s," *Journal of International Affairs* 40, 2 (Winter/Spring 1987), table 1, p. 239.

9. Ibid., p. 240.

10. See Chong Lim Kim, "Potential for Democratic Change in a Divided Nation," in Kim and Kihl, *Political Change,* pp. 44–72.

11. See Young Whan Kihl, "South Korea's Search for a New Order: An Overview," in ibid., pp. 10–15.

12. Kim Jae Won, *Subcontracting Market Expansion and Subcontracting Activities Promotion: The Case of Korea's Machine Industry* (Seoul: Korea Development Institute, 1983), p. 43.

13. Wonmo Dong, "Student Activism and the Presidential Politics of 1987 in South Korea," in Kim and Kihl, *Political Change,* pp. 171, 177.

14. See World Bank, *Korea: The Small and Medium Machinery Industry Project Staff Appraisal Report* (1979, mimeo).

15. Dong, "Student Activism," pp. 178–179.

16. Dilip Mukerjee, *Lessons from Korea's Industrial Experience* (Kuala Lumpur: Institute for Strategic and International Studies, 1986), pp. 70–71.

17. See, for example, Kim Dae-jung, *Mass Participatory Economy: A Democratic Alternative for Korea* (Lanham, Md.: University Press of America, 1985), and *Prison Writings* (Berkeley: University of California Press, 1987).

18. See Kinney, "Students, Intellectuals, and the Churches," pp. 180–195; and Sung Chul Yang, "Student Political Activism: The Case of the April

Revolution in South Korea," *Youth and Society* 5, 1 (September 1973), pp. 47–60.

19. Dong, "University Students," pp. 238, 244–245, 250.

20. Ibid., p. 246.

21. Hang Yul Rhee, "The Economic Problems of the Korean Political Economy," in Kim and Kihl, *Political Change*, pp. 191, 196–197, 202; Edward S. Mason et al., *The Economic and Social Modernization of the Republic of Korea* (Cambridge: Harvard University Press, 1980), ch. 12 and pp. 481–484; and L. L. Wade and B. S. Kim, *The Political Economy of Success: Public Policy and Economic Development in the Republic of Korea* (Seoul: Kyung Hee University, 1977), table 2.9, p. 80.

22. See Myungsoon Shin, "Political Protest and Government Decision Making: Korea, 1945–1972," *American Behavioral Scientist* 26, 3 (January-February 1983), pp. 395–416; and Barry Renfrew, "Radical Students Again Rampage Through Seoul, Battle Riot Police," *Washington Times*, 13 June 1988, p. A8.

23. Dong, "Student Activism," pp. 175, 181.

24. See "Will Success Spoil the Korean Church?," pp. 39–40.

25. See Cardinal Kim Soo Hwan, "Nine Day Repentence Sermon," Myongdong Cathedral, 15 March 1987 (mimeo).

26. See Ralph M. Clough, *Embattled Korea: The Rivalry for International Support* (Boulder: Westview, 1987), pp. 104–107, 179–184.

27. Peter Almond, "North Korea Places Missiles Near DMZ," *Washington Times*, 7 June 1988, p. A1; Mike Breen, "Invasion Fears Are Raised by S. Korea," ibid., 16 June 1988, p. A7; Breen, "South Koreans Still Fear a Surprise Attack," ibid., 27 June 1988, p. A8; and Bill Gertz, "Soviets Add Advanced Jets to North Korean Buildup," ibid., 22 June 1988, p. A5.

28. Kim Il-sung, *Report to the Sixth Congress of the Workers' Party of Korea on the Work of the Central Committee, October 10, 1980* (Pyongyang: Foreign Languages, 1980), pp. 64–65.

29. Edward Neilson, "Police in Seoul Battle Students in Major Clash," *Washington Times*, 10 June 1988, p. A1.

30. K. Connie Kang, "Anti-U.S. Feelings Grow in S. Korea," *San Francisco Examiner*, 5 June 1988, p. A14.

31. "Anti-U.S. Feelings Grow in S. Korea," *Washington Times*, 22 June 1988, p. A2.

32. "Kim Dae-jung Scores U.S. Role in Korea," ibid., 2 June 1988, p. A2.

33. "Korea: A New Target for the Church Left" and "Korea: IRD Special Report," in *Religion and Democracy*, September/October 1988, pp. 1–12.

34. As quoted in Clough, *Embattled Korea*, p. 181.

## Chapter Six

1. "Moving Cautiously in Liberalizing Farm Sectors, Minister Says," *Korea Digest* 2, 1 (February 1988), p. 6.

2. Richard Halloran, "Weinberger Says U.S. Will Maintain Curbs on Seoul's Sales of Arms," *New York Times*, 1 April 1982, p. A8.

3. See Nack An and Rose An, "North Korea Military Assistance," in John F. Copper and Daniel S. Papp, eds., *Communist Nations' Military Assistance*

(Boulder: Westview, 1983); and Clyde Haberman, "North Korea Reported to Step Up Arms Sales and Training Abroad," *New York Times,* 24 November 1983, p. A1.

4. Young Whan, *Policies and Politics in Divided Korea: Regimes in Contest* (Boulder: Westview, 1984), p. 190.

5. See *Korea at the Crossroads: Implications for American Policy* (Washington: Council on Foreign Relations, 1987), ch. 4.

6. As cited in *Korea Digest* 2, 1 (February 1988), p. 2.

7. See Douglas Pike and Benjamin Ward, "Losing and Winning: Korea and Vietnam as Success Stories," *Washington Quarterly* 10, 2 (Summer 1987), pp. 77–85.

# Index of Names

Afghanistan, 110, 113
Africa, 9, 39
Anglo-Japanese Treaty, 7
ASEAN, 111
Association of South East Asian Nations, 111
Australia, 78

Bolsheviks, 10, 44
Britain, 6–9
Buddhism, 1
Burma, 99

Canada, 99, 108
Carter, President Jimmy, 35, 59, 72, 100
Castro, Fidel, 46, 60
Catholicism, 97
*chaebol*, 59, 89, 90
Chang Myon, 29, 55
China, 1, 2, 4, 6, 10, 22, 23, 26, 34, 50, 52, 56, 59, 63–67, 68, 70, 71, 80, 81, 109
Choi Chang-yoon, 105
Choi Kyu-hah, 35
Chollima, 19
Chong-bok, 51
Chorwon, 70
Chosun, 1, 2
Chosun Dynasty: see Yi Dynasty
Christianity, 85, 95, 97
Chun Doo-hwan, 35, 57, 86–90, 99, 100
*Communist Manifesto*, 43
Confucianism, 1, 9
Cuba, 23, 46, 68

Democratic Justice Party, 87, 96
Democratic People's Republic of Korea (DPRK): economics, 19–21, 23, 27–30, 38; history, 5, 13, 15–18; military

threats, 64–68, 70–77, 80; politics, 46–51, 54–56, 58, 59

East Asia, 1, 2, 4, 24, 59, 65, 66, 72, 78–80, 82, 98, 109, 112
Eastern Europe, 9
East Germany, 38
Economic Planning Board, 32, 56
Engels, Friedrich, 43–45

Federation of Economic Organizations and Korean Industries, 89
Federation of Industries, 96
Federation of Korean Medium and Small Businesses, 89
Five Year Plan, 56
France, 6, 9, 54

Generalized System of Preferences (GSP), 106, 107
Geneva conference, 67
Germany, 6, 9, 63, 65
Gorbachev, Mikhail, 79
Guam Doctrine, 34, 72, 78

Han River, 1
Honda, 36
Hong Kong, 25
Hungary, 23
Hyundai Electronic, 36
Hyundai Motor Company, 36

Inchon, 78, 90
India, 110
Indonesia, 59
Industrial Revolution, 42
Iran, 107
Israel, 108
Italy, 54

125

# INDEX OF NAMES

Jaisohn, Philip, 53
Japan, 2–8, 12–14, 24, 26, 36, 52, 53, 59, 60, 63, 66, 78, 79, 81
Japan, Sea of, 2
*juche*, 10, 67

Kampuchea, 103, 110
Kanghwa, Treaty of, 6
Kennan, George, 5
Khrushchev, Nikita, 69
Kim Dae-jung, 86, 87, 90, 101
Kim Il-sung, 10, 11, 14, 15, 19, 21, 46–48, 50, 64, 66–70, 76
Kim Jong-il, 76
Kim Young-sam, 86, 87, 90
Komundo, 7
Korea Chamber of Commerce, 89
Korea Development Institute, 92
Korean Technology Development Corporation, 36
Korean Trade Promotion Corporation, 32
Korean Workers' Party, 11, 47, 48, 68, 81
Koryo, 1
Kuomintang, 26

Land Reform Act, 26
Laos, 103, 110
Latin America, 9, 39
Lenin, V. I., 10, 44, 63
Liang Ch'i-ch'ao (Liang Qichao), 52, 53
Liberal Party, 28
Liu Shaoqi, 63, 64

MacArthur, Douglas, 26
Mahan, Afred Thayer, 4, 5
Malaysia, 59
Manchuria, 3, 8
Manila, 110
Mao Zedong, 3, 10, 15, 23, 63, 64, 83
Marx, Karl, 43–45
Marxism-Leninism, 10, 12, 14, 15, 19, 22, 23, 27, 30, 34, 38, 43–47, 51, 90, 95
Meiji, 7, 9, 13, 52
Ministry of Education (ROK), 86
Ministry of Public Security (DPRK), 49
Ministry of State Enterprises (ROK), 56
Minjung, 97
Mongols, 1, 2

Najin, 80
National Assembly, 29, 86, 91
National Conference for Unification, 35
National Council for Science and Technology, 36

National Federation of Student Associations, 86
New Community Movement, 31
Nixon, President Richard, 34, 72
Nixon-Sato communique, 112
North Korea: *see* Democratic People's Republic of Korea

Olympic Games, 87

Paekche, 1
Panmunjom, 70
Park Chung-hee, 29–33, 35, 55–57, 69, 70
Philippines, 52, 77
Portsmouth Peace Conference, 8
Protestantism, 97
Pukchang, 109
Pusan, 90, 93

Rangoon, 75
Reagan, President Ronald, 78
Republic of Korea (ROK): economics, 20, 25–39; history, 5, 12–18; military threats, 64–66, 69–77, 79, 81; politics, 51, 54–61
Revolutionary Party for Reunification, 99
Rha Woong-bae, 105
Rhee, Syngman, 14, 25, 27, 28, 31, 54, 95
Roh Tae-woo, 87, 90, 91, 100
Rosen/Nishi Convention, 7
Russia, 4, 6–10

Saemaul Undong, 31
Samsung Semiconductor and Telecommunications, 36
Scandinavia, 18
SCUD missiles, 76
Seoul, 5, 15, 28
Seven Year Plan, 23
Siberia, 2, 3
*Silhak* movement, 53
Silla, 1
Singapore, 25, 59
Sino-Soviet relations, 23, 68, 99
SMI (Small and Medium Sized Industries), 89, 92, 93, 106
So Che-pil (Philip Jaisohn), 53
*Sohak*, 51
Southern Europe, 9
South Korea: *see* Republic of Korea
Soviet Union, 3–6, 11, 14, 15, 20, 23, 45–46, 61, 63–65, 67–71, 74–83, 99, 100, 109, 110, 111–113

## INDEX OF NAMES  127

Stalin, Josef, 10, 11, 15, 20, 24, 44–46, 50, 63, 68, 83
Sun Yat-sen, 26, 52
Supreme People's Assembly, 48

T'aebaeksan Mountains, 5
Taegu, 90, 93
Taiwan, 4, 25, 26, 34, 51, 56, 59, 65, 78
Thailand, 59
Third Party Congress, 47
*Tongnip Sinmun*, 7
Toyota, 36
Truman, President Harry, 65
Tsushima Straight, 79
Tung-i, 1
Twentieth Party Congress, 68

Unggi, 109
United Nations, 14, 65, 67, 109
United States Chamber of Commerce, 96
United States Information Service, 96

Vietnam, 23, 34, 51, 59, 68, 71, 72, 103, 113
Vladivostok, 79

Western Europe, 9, 24, 42, 60
West Germany, 38, 76
Workers' Party of Korea: *see* Korean Workers' Party
World Bank, 33, 93
World War I, 9, 10, 38,
World War II, 3, 10, 11, 63–65, 78, 100

Yalu River, 71
Yellow Sea, 2
Yi (Chosun) Dynasty, 2, 7, 29, 51
Yi Ik, 51
Yi Song-gye, 2
Yi Sung-man, 14
Yun Po-sun, 28
Yushin Constitution, 34

Zhou Enlai, 70
Zimbabwe, 107

ASHEVILLE-BUNCOMBE
TECHNICAL COMMUNITY COLLEGE
3 3312 00037 1039